SECONDARY SCHOOL TEACHER EDUCATION IN TRANSITION

THE UNIVERSITY OF MICHIGAN/INDIAN UNIVERSITIES
EXCHANGE PROGRAM

SECONDARY SCHOOL TEACHER EDUCATION IN TRANSITION

JOHN P. LIPKIN

ASIA PUBLISHING HOUSE
LONDON

ISBN 0.210.22670.6

PRINTED IN INDIA
AT ANANDA PRESS, LUCKNOW AND PUBLISHED BY P. S. JAYASINGHE, ASIA PUBLISHING HOUSE, 447 STRAND, LONDON WC 2

FOREWORD

THE UNIVERSITY of Michigan/Indian Universities Exchange Project is proud to present the first monograph in the Indian Education Series. This and the second volume concern teacher education in Bombay and Gujarat, respectively. The third monograph, deals with student organisations in Indian higher education. Four others presently in preparation by the authors will relate to secondary vocational education, advanced technological education, the national discipline scheme, and teacher education for village primary and secondary schools.

Each of these monographs is a dissertation produced originally as a part of the requirement for the Ph.D. degree. The author of each spent at least an academic year in India to conduct field work for his project.

The financial support which made possible the year of field activity as well as the publication of the studies has come from grants made by the United States Department of State and the United States Office of Education under the terms of Public Law 480. For the academic and field programs of all but two of the young scholars, National Defence Education Act Fellowships in Comparative Education have provided necessary support.

The members of educational institutions associated with the Exchange Project have supported every aspect of the process which culminates in these studies. They have provided guidance, transportation, housing, and friendship for faculty and student consultants and researchers. They have possessed the understanding of education and society in India and the United States indispensable in the planning and execution of project activities.

The University of Michigan/Indian Universities Exchange Project was initiated in the late months of 1962 in association with leaders at the University of Baroda and the University of Bombay. In January of 1966 the National Council for Educational Research and Training at New Delhi joined the group.

From the outset, the members of the institutions engaged in the project have sought means to assist each other. The faculty and the student body of the School of Education at the University of

v

Michigan have greatly appreciated the insight and information provided by the visiting professors who have come to Ann Arbor each academic year since 1962. They have been happy to receive assurances from Baroda and Bombay that the professors and advanced students who have joined staffs in these centers have made valuable contributions to the study of society and education in India.

The present study and those to follow are additions to the already available publications issued by the Comparative Education Program and prepared by the visiting Indian professors and staff members at Ann Arbor. All are available without change upon request.

Special thanks go to Professors William M. Cave and W. Robert Dixon of the University of Michigan School of Education and Professor L. A. Peter Gosling of the University's Department of Geography for their sponsorship of the present study.

Claude A. Eggertsen
Editor

PREFACE

THE UNIVERSITY provides the student with the intellectual resources necessary for carrying out his thesis task. The University of Michigan and Bombay University were bountiful providers, and I humbly acknowledge my debt to these institutions.

The most highly valued asset of any university is its personnel; those who administer, teach and share the often times lonely pursuit of knowledge. In Bombay, the University's Rector, Dr. G. D. Parikh, and the principals of Bombay University's three training colleges, Dr. N. R. Parasnis of Secondary Training College, Reverend A. Solagran of St. Xavier's Institute of Education, and Dr. N. N. Shukla of the Sadhna Institute of Educational Research and Training, were all of immeasurable assistance. I must also express my appreciation to the faculty and students of the three training colleges and, in particular, my adopted adviser, Prof. M.Y. Bhide.

My wife, Catherine, and I are grateful to all those in India whose hospitality and help we enjoyed. The encouragement and counsel of the late Professor Puttaparti Sreenivasachar of Omsania University is also gratefully recalled.

At the University of Michigan, Professor Claude Eggertsen initiated the exchange with Bombay and Baroda Universities, which made this study possible, and served as my guide and mentor.

John P. Lipkin

CONTENTS

APPENDICES

LIST OF TABLES

CHAPTER I

THE ADAPTATION OF THE BRITISH EDUCATIONAL TRADITION IN BOMBAY

THE PUBLICATION of the *Report of the Secondary Education Commission*[1] in 1953 marked the beginning of a new era in Indian secondary education. No longer were the traditional hallmarks of the English language and literary subjects to dominate the secondary schools which, heretofore, were seen almost exclusively as an avenue to the university for the socially and intellectually elite. The keynote of India's secondary education was to be functionality with respect to India's social and economic plans; the academic high schools were to be replaced by multipurpose, comprehensive high schools with an expanded student base and a broadened curriculum in order to prepare all of India's youth for civic and vocational competency.

The reforms envisioned for India's secondary education naturally required corresponding changes in the training of secondary teachers. The main purpose of this study is to determine the extent and the causes of the transition of secondary teacher training from the academic pattern introduced by the British to a pattern more suited to the Indian societal context. The major hypothesis is that Bombay University's secondary teacher training colleges have undergone certain changes as a result of India's efforts to adapt its educational institutions to national plans for development, in general, and the city of Bombay's commercial and industrial development, in particular. The major impetus for this change was brought about by India's acquisition of independence from Great Britain in 1947, although the control and the content of education throughout the British period had become increasingly oriented to the Indian society.

---

[1] India, Ministry of Education, *Report of the Secondary Education Commission, 1952-53* (Mudaliar Report), (5th reprint; Delhi: Government of India Publications 1962).

As guidelines for assessing the changes in the training colleges four categories or dimensions of reform based on the recommendations of the *Report of the Secondary Education Commission* have been determined :

1. The training college curriculum is being broadened and revised. Technical subjects are being included along with the standard academic offerings, and the syllabus is being brought up to date to include advances in the scientific and social scientific disciplines relevant to the Indian context.

2. Less formal and more diversified methods are being employed to supplement the lecture, which has been the standard fare for the theoretical portion of the curriculum in the training colleges.

3. The quality of instruction is being improved by means of higher standards of selectivity of the training candidates and training colleges faculty members and the development of the advanced study of education.

4. The training colleges are enlarging their immediate sphere of influence by providing the in-service teacher training required to bring about the secondary school reform envisioned by the *Report of the Secondary Education Commission*.

This study does not purport to investigate the economic, social, or political problems of India or the city of Bombay, although such studies are consulted and the findings of certain authors are accepted when they are relevant. Rather, the essential point of view is that before the broader question of education's contribution to a particular society can be adjudged, the educational system, itself, must be the object of thoughtful inquiry.

An implicit assumption of this study is that education can contribute to the progress of a nation, and that this progress, based on the human capacity to benefit from the experiences of the past, can be measured in terms of the attainment of ever changing goals.[2] The most fundamental goal in India is the economic development necessary to provide adequate living standards for all of its inhabitants, and the attainment of this goal requires productively employed technologically skilled personnel.

---

[2] E. H. Carr, *What is History ?* (London : Pelican Books edition, 1964), p. 119.

The appearance of two noteworthy publications in 1963, James Conant's *The Education of American Teachers* and *The Education and Training of Teachers, The Year Book of Education, 1963,* signify the convergence of interest in this topic both in the United States and abroad. Although a major study of Indian teacher training has not yet appeared, numerous pamphlets have been published under the national government's auspices in the past decade. T. K. N. Menon and G. N. Kaul's *Experiments in Teacher Training* and K. L. Shrimali's *Better Teacher Education* both published in 1954, ushered forth this wave of interest which was largely prompted by the Secondary Education Commission's Report in 1954.

In addition to these pamphlets several of the Master's theses written in Bombay University have dealt with the secondary teacher and his training, but neither the pamphlets nor the theses have provided the investigator with more than a non-interpretative account of past developments or the repetitious descriptions of the shortcomings of the training institutions.

In approaching Indian education one is reminded of Lovat Fraser's observation that, "No topic has been written upon so interminably or as a rule with so little profit,"[3] but such a spirit cannot be permitted to prevail over the intentions of those who would begin afresh. The researcher will find considerable material in the form of the central government's official educational accounts and reports which have been written throughout the British period and have continued to appear since India has become independent. Of special value are the reports of the national educational bodies which have been commissioned to investigate the general state of education or a particular phase of education on a national basis and to make recommendations for guiding future educational policies. These documents, from Macaulay's Minute of 1835 to the *Report of the Secondary Education Commission* in 1953, have perused from the point of view of their relevance to the issues surrounding secondary teacher training.

In addition to the central government's documents, yearly educational reports at the state level were available as well as the records of Bombay University and its affiliated secondary training colleges. Although these records are not as carefully compiled or stored as

---

[3] Lovat Fraser, *India Under Curzon and After*, (London : William Heinemann, 1911), p. 180.

would be desired, they nonetheless constitute an essential source of information, particularly for tracing the history of the training colleges.

There have not been any major interpretative works on secondary teacher training in India or the impact of the *Report of the Secondary Education Commission*. However, several Indian sources relating to education in general are available. The most useful of of these are the general histories of Indian education and the history of education in Bombay State and Bombay University. Particularly noteworthy works in each of these categories include Syed Nurullah and J. P. Naik's *A History of Education in India, A Review of Education in Bombay State* edited by J. P. Naik and *A History of the University of Bombay* by S. R. Dongerkerry.

The social scientist faced with the task of analyzing foreign institutions is grateful for the relevant studies of other Western observers even when these studies do not deal directly with the investigator's chief concern. In this connection Edward A. Shils' *The Intellectual between Tradition and Modernity* and Margaret L. Cormack's *She Who Rides a Peacock*, although primarily dealing with the Indian intellectual and female respectively, have provided valuable insights into many of the problems relevant to Indian secondary teacher training.

While published sources furnished the necessary information regarding the development of secondary teacher training and documented India's educational goals, they did not provide the investigator with the material needed to analyze the present efforts of Bombay University's training colleges to achieve these goals. For this purpose the following means were employed :

1. Questionnaire—closed form questionnaires were administered to the students of Bombay University's training colleges after administering a trial questionnaire to the students at the training college in Punjim, Goa.

2. Interviews—the faculty members and headmasters of Bombay University's training colleges participated in an oral interview of approximately one hour's duration. Interviews were also conducted with various members of Bombay University's faculty and staff, the principals and teachers of various secondary schools throughout Bombay and educational officials in the State Department of Public Instruction and the National Ministry of Education in New Delhi.

3. Observation—approximately twenty of the training college lectures were attended and the entire range of practical training was observed, including the practice lessons given by the trainees in various secondary schools surrounding the training colleges. Also various conferences, faculty meetings, exhibitions and demonstrations in the training colleges and the university were attended.

With the increasing recognition of the strategic positions of secondary teacher training in a comprehensive scheme of educational development such as that presently embarked upon by the Indian nation, the need for a thorough understanding of the existing training institutions should be apparent. Through this examination of Bombay University's progress as measured against prescribed national goals, an understanding of the complexities involved in the implementation of these goals can be achieved.

Indian institutions are conditioned or influenced by the past to an extent that the Westerner, accustomed as he is to change, would have difficulty in appreciating. In attempting to understand the present training colleges and their likely future path, an understanding of the manner in which the British system of education originated and evolved in India is therefore essential.

Neither the establishment of the first Western settlement in Bombay by the Portuguese in 1534[4] nor its cession to Great Britain in 1661[5] resulted in any alteration of its small fishing village character. Not until the unsuccessful Indian National Revolt of 1857, or the Mutiny as the British termed it, and the resultant transfer of power from the British East India Company to the British Crown, were the foundations of today's commercial and industrial center established.[6]

The status of native, or indigenous education as it is commonly referred to, was at a particularly low level throughout India at the beginning of the nineteenth century.[7] This low state of education,

---

[4] *Imperial Gazeteer of India* (New Edition ; Oxford : Clarendon Press, 1908), III, p. 286.

[5] A.R. Ingram, *The Gateway to India* (London : Oxford University Press, 1938), p. 153.

[6] Thomas R. Metcalf, *The Aftermath of Revolt, India, 1857-1870* (Princeton : Princeton University Press, 1964), p. 6.

[7] S.N. Mukerji, *History of Education in India (Modern Period)* (4th ed. ; Baroda, India : Acharya Book Depot, 1961), p. 4.

in turn, was one aspect of the general decadence of Indian civili-
zation which marked this period and helped to account for the
inability of India to resist the establishment of British rule.[8]

A survey of Bombay's education in 1827 revealed the absence of
any schools of learning, as India's centers for the study of the
Hindu religion were called. It can reasonably be assumed that
such higher learning as took place was carried out on an informal,
oral basis by the Brahmin priests.

Organized education at this time was restricted to the native schools,
which imparted a rudimentary knowledge of reading, writing and
arithmetic on a strictly utilitarian basis for trading purposes.[9]

The first efforts of the British to educate the native population were
initiated by Montstuart Elphinstone, the Governor of the Province
of Bombay. Through his efforts, the Bombay Native Education
Society was formed which founded the Central English School in
1824, thus marking the advent of Western education in Bombay.[10]

Considerable controversy arose concerning the manner in which
the English should educate the natives. What should be taught,
who should be taught, and what was to be the purpose of the education ? These questions were centered around still another query—
that of the choice of an appropriate medium of instruction.

In deciding upon language policy, the English agreed that
instruction beyond the most elementary level could not be imparted in the vernacular languages because of their low level of development. The choice of language was therefore restricted to English
or one of the Oriental languages; Sanskrit, Arabic and Persian.
Since Sanskrit was the language employed by the Hindus in their
higher learning, and the Muslims used Arabic or Persian, the
decision to use English represented a neutral choice with respect to
religious background.[11]

[8] A.L. Basham, *The Wonder That Was India* (New York : Grove Press, Inc.,
1959), p. 481.

[9] H.S. Sharp (ed.), *Selections from Educational Records : Part I, 1781-1839* (Calcutta : Superintendent Government Printing, 1920), p. 198.

[10] J.P. Naik (ed.), *A Review of Education in Bombay State* (Poona, India :
Government of Bombay, 1958), p. 4. This Central English School later deve-
loped into Bombay's well-known Elphinstone High School and Elphinstone
College.

[11] Gostha Behari Kanungo, *The Language Controversy in Indian Education : An
Historical Study* (Chicago: University of Chicago, Comparative Education Center,
1962), p. 6.

J. S. Furnivall has convincingly demonstrated the correlation between the need for English usage for higher learning and the increasing opportunity for Indian employment in administrative positions. He suggests that the renewal of the charter of the East India Company in 1833, which virtually assured the continued assignment of administrative posts to Indians without discrimination provided that they knew the English languages resulted in the final establishment of English as the teaching medium.[12]

From Furnivall's point of view, the decision to use the English medium, embodied in Macaulay's Minute of 1835,[13] merely attached official government sanction to an already irrevocable position. While this view has definite merit, it tends to underestimate the significance of the controversy between the Anglicists and Orientalists, both of whom were vying for the British government's support. The resolution of this debate in favor of the Anglicists was at least in part attributable to the government's view that instruction in English could result in a unified approach to native learning, the economic argument of Furnivall notwithstanding.

Along with the decision to use English, two very important concomitant results stemmed from Macaulay's Minute, which was given the force of law by India's ruling officer, Lord Bentinck.[14] The first was the decision to promote the literature and science of Europe, and the second, an indirect effect of the Minute, was the establishment of secular education in India. The use of English diminished the prospects for the flourishing of either the Hindu or the Muslim religions or the Christian religion within the framework of the English educational system. In order to compete successfully for students with the English schools it became necessary for the Christian missionary schools to redirect their emphasis from proselytizing to preparing their students for the British type of higher learning.[15]

To this day controversy exists regarding the motives of Great Britain in establishing an English form of education in India. The

---

[12] J. S. Furnivall, *Educational Progress in Southeast Asia* (New York : International Secretariat, Institute of Pacific Relations, 1943), p. 20.

[13] T. B. Macaulay, "Minute by Honorable T. B. Macaulay dated the 2nd February, 1835," *Selections from Educational Records : Part I, 1781-1839*, p. 116.

[14] Lord William Bentinck, "Lord Bentinck's Resolution of the 7th March, 1835," *Selections from Educational Records : Part I, 1781-1839*, p. 116.

[15] G. D. Parikh, *General Education and Indian Universities* (Bombay : Asia Publishing House, 1959), p. 119.

Indian point of view, stated in the extreme, holds that in order to make their conquest of India complete, the English sought to dominate the Indians culturally as well as politically and economically. Contrarily, the British, following the arguments of Macaulay, assert that the goal of Western education was the elevation of Indian society and, although the members reached directly by this education were of practical necessity limited, those recipients of a Western education were encouraged to study their own languages in order that they might spread this knowledge throughout the native population.[16]

While the question of the nature of the education to be imparted in India was resolved, that of the form it was to take remained to be defined. It is to this general question that Wood Education Despatch of 1854 was addressed. Not only is this document of vital importance for the pattern of secondary and higher education that it established, but it also reveals the attitude of the time toward the training of secondary teachers.

The Despatch proposed that universities, modeled after London University, be established for the purpose of conducting examinations and conferring degrees. These universities were not to have a teaching function but were designed to insure adequate standards and uniformity in the colleges. Upon demonstrating to the university adequate facilities, a properly qualified staff and adherence to the prescribed curriculum, the colleges became affiliated to the university for degree purposes. The Despatch further advocated the establishment of a matriculation examination to be taken at the end of the secondary school level which would serve as the basis for judging college entrance qualifications.[17]

As a direct result of this Despatch, Bombay University was established as one of India's original universities in 1857.[18] The two

[16] A complete exposition of the Indian point of view can be found in B. K. Boman-Behram, *Educational Controversies in India* (Bombay: D. B. Taraporevala and Sons and Co., 1943). For the British side of the argument consult Arthur Mayhew, *The Education of India* (London: Faber and Gwyer, 1926).

[17] Great Britain, "A Copy of a Despatch to the Government of India on the Subject of General Education in India," Dated July 19th, 1854, printed in *Return of Sums Spent on Native Education in India Since 1834* (Facts of Publication not given), p. 10. This document was obtained from the Bombay University Library.

[18] The other original universities, also established in 1857, were Calcutta and Madras Universities.

colleges affiliated to Bombay University at the outset, the Elphinstone Institute and Grant Medical College, offered instruction in the Arts, Law, Engineering and Medicine.[19]

The second major result of the Despatch was the creation of a Department of Public Instruction for the State of Bombay.[20] This Department was created in order to provide the administrative machinery for administering grants to the secondary schools. Under this system, which has continued to the present, educational inspectors of the Department of Public Instruction approved or granted official recognition to the secondary schools which met the qualifications prescribed by the state. The intent of these grants, which were based on a percentage of the funds expended by each secondary institution, was to encourage the local private management of secondary education.

From the outset of higher Western Education in India, little attention was paid to teaching methods or techniques on the secondary level.[21] Since in England the training of secondary teachers did not really become established until the end of the nineteenth century [22] it is not surprising that such training was not considered necessary, particularly since the Indian secondary schools were originally staffed by Englishmen.

As the number of secondary schools began to increase, the supply of teachers from England could no longer meet the demand, and the need for staffing the schools with Indians became apparent. In order to meet the demand for teachers at both the secondary and primary levels, Wood's Despatch recommended the introduction of the Lancasterian method whereby senior pupils would carry out the introduction under the supervision of a master teacher.[23]

This method had the advantage of bringing a large number of students together for instruction at a small cost, but in its limited application in the Bombay English schools, the senior pupils

[19] Sunderao Ramras Dongerkerry, *A History of the University of Bombay* (Bombay: University of Bombay, 1957), p. 6.

[20] Syed Nurullah and J. P. Naik, *A History of Education in India*, (rev. ed.; Bombay: Macmillan and Co., Ltd., 1950) p. 206.

[21] B. B. Misra, *The Indian Middle Classes*, (London: Oxford University Press, 1961), p. 186.

[22] Sir Philip Magnus, *Educational Aims and Efforts, 1880-1910*, (London: Longmans Green and Co., 1910), p. 23.

[23] Great Britain, "A Copy of a Despatch to the Government of India on the Subject of General Education in India," p. 12.

predictably did not prove adequate to the task of imparting instruction at the secondary level. In order to provide instruction which
would insure that the students would meet the university-prescribed standards for college entrance, secondary teachers with higher
qualifications than experience in the Lancasterian method were
required.

The advocacy by the Wood's Despatch of the Lancasterian
method signifies an educational dilemma which persisted in an
acute form throughout the history of colonial India; namely, how
to accommodate large numbers of students and maintain high
standards simultaneously. The implementation of the type of education decided upon in Macaulay's Minute meant that only a
small portion of the Indian population could aspire to an education beyond the primary level. If education was to be spread
throughout the nation, change was required, and the institution of
the university-prescribed matriculation examination as the badge
of success left little or no room for flexibility in the curriculum at
the secondary level.

In addition to the Lancasterian method, Wood's Despatch
advocated the establishment of normal schools in order to bring
about an adequate supply of teachers.[24] Although this recommendation did not result in the establishment of such institutions, it
nonetheless could be considered the earliest harbinger of training
colleges. Acting on the advice of the Despatch, Department of
Public Instruction for the State of Bombay proposed the establishment of two training colleges, but the Government of India, citing
its desire for a more gradual approach, did not allot the required
funds.[25]

In order to ensure a minimum standard for teacher's qualifications, in 1869 the Department of Public Instruction required a
certificate of competency of all of the teachers in the government
English schools who did not possess university degrees. However,
no formal training was required for this certificate, and only in a
few of the government's schools was any special effort made to
prepare the teachers for the state inspector's examination which
led to certification.

The prevailing view in 1869 echoed by Sir Alexander Grant,

[24] *Ibid.*, pp. 12-13.
[25] *Report of the Director of Public Instruction, 1856-57* (Bombay: Education Society's Press, 1859, pp. 17-18.

Bombay's Director of Public Instruction, was that, "The university was the great normal school."[26] Grant, however, did believe that teacher training was necessary for those without a university degree and, hence, reiterated the recommendation of Wood's Despatch that normal schools be established for the training of non-graduates.[27]

The wish of those favoring pedagogical training for all teachers first received official recognition in the Report of the Indian Education Commission of 1882 known as the Hunter Commission Report. This report, a landmark in Indian teacher training history, espoused the view that training in pedagogical principles, even for university graduates, was desirable.[28]

In view of the absence of any training institutions in Bombay, the Hunter Commission recommended that the professional training of teachers be carried out in the best high schools under the tutelage of the schools' headmasters.[29] A second means by which teachers could become qualified, also advocated by the Commission, was through an examination in the principles and practice of teaching.[30] This suggestion was adopted by Bombay in 1899, when the Department of Public Instruction instituted the Secondary Teacher's Certificate Examination.[31] The examination consisted of a practical part in which the candidate's ability in an actual classroom situation was evaluated as well as an examination on the theory of teaching. Teachers in government schools or schools recognized by the state government, whether secondary graduates or university graduates, were eligible for the examination.[32]

The Secondary Teacher's Certificate Examination served Bombay in lieu of a formal training program during a period in which regular training institutions were increasing in number and acade-

[26] D. M. Sidhwa, "The Training of Secondary Teachers in the State of Bombay" (unpublished Master's thesis, Bombay University, 1951), pp. 8-9.

[27] Ibid.

[28] India, Report of the Indian Education Commission, February 3, 1882, (Calcutta: Government of India. 1933), p. 235.

[29] Ibid., p. 237.

[30] Ibid., p. 236.

[31] K. S. Vakil, History of Training of Teachers, (Kolhapur: Shri Maharani Tarabai Teacher's College, n. d.), pp. 12-13.

[32] Sidhwa, "The Training of Secondary Teachers in the State of Bombay," p. 12.

mic respectability, both in England and in India. As a body of
pedagogical knowledge and skills developed which was capable of
being imparted to students to make them more effective classroom
teachers, the principle that all teachers should be trained gradually
won widespread, albeit not universal, acceptance.[33]

By 1902, Bombay was the only state without an institution for
training secondary teachers.[34] This is particularly surprising when
the fact that the State of Bombay had one of India's original universities is taken into consideration. The creation of Bombay University
provided for the development of new colleges, and as these institutions were established and grew, the need for the parallel development of secondary schools, necessary for the preparation of
college entrants occurred.[35] The great demands that were thus
placed on the secondary schools, which were the necessary path to
the university degree and subsequent remunerative employment,
called for highly qualified secondary teachers.

This need for capable secondary teachers was recognized by the
teachers themselves, but their requests for a training program were
not fulfilled by the Department of Public Instruction, which cited
the lack of funds and inadequate standards of English on the part
of the non-university graduates, who would be entering the program, as grounds for their inaction.[36] Neither did a further recommendation from the Government of India in 1887, this time citing
teacher training as a remedy for the growing problem of student
"indiscipline", produce the desired results.[37]

The necessary driving force for establishing a secondary training
institution in Bombay finally arrived in the person of Lord Curzon,
who began his dynamic administration as India's Governor General in 1899. Curzon believed that a matter as vital to India's

[33] S. J. Curtis and M. S. Boultwood, *History of English Education Since 1800* (London: University Tutorial Press, 1960), p. 221.

The tenets of Johann Herbart, the luminary of Europe's sociopsychological movement, were introduced into England in 1897 with the publication of John Adam's work, *The Herbartian Psychology Applied to Education*.

[34] Nurullah and Naik, *A History of Education in India*, p. 307.

[35] Bruce Tiebout McCully, *English Education and the Origins of Indian National-ism* (New York: Columbia University Press, 1940), p. 150.

[26] *The Bombay Educational Record and Journal*, XXI, No. 2 (August, 1898), p. 61.

[27] Sidhwa, "The Training of Secondary Teachers in the State of Bombay," p. 10.

welfare as education should come under the aegis of the central government.[38] Accordingly, he created the post of Director-General of Education and established a policy of increased financial aid to education and its attendant, increased central control.[39]

In his Resolution in 1904, Curzon laid great stress on the training of secondary teachers as a means for increasing the supply of teachers and ultimately improving the quality of secondary instruction, which he noted had become too mechanical owing to an overemphasis on notes, textbooks and examinations. Observing that the existing secondary training colleges in other states had helped to achieve these ends, Curzon stated that the time had come for Bombay to establish such an institution.[40]

As a result of Curzon's directive and a grant of 600,000 rupees (Rs.600,000=$120,000),[41] the Secondary Training College was established in Bombay in 1906.[42]

After a visit to the United Kingdom for the purpose of observing teacher training institutions, J. Nelson Fraser, a former professor of English literature at Deccan College, became the first principal of Bombay's training college. The first class was comprised of seventeen graduate and twelve non-graduate teachers. The staff consisted of Fraser, who taught the literary subjects, and a vice-principal who taught the pedagogical subjects.[43]

At the outset, the training was primarily focused on teaching methods or techniques. The faculty gave demonstration lessons and then criticized the practice lessons given by the students. The pedagogical subjects offered included elocution, drawing, the history of education, and the psychology of education, while English

[38] Fraser, *India Under Curzon and After*, p. 183. From a speech given by Curzon at the convocation of Calcutta University in February, 1900.

[39] Naik, *A Review of Education in Bombay State*, p. 17.

[40] India, "Indian Educational Policy Resolution of the Government of India in the Home Department," (Calcutta, March 11, 1904), *Progress of Education in India, 1897-98; 1901-02* (Calcutta: Director General of Education in India, n.d.), pp. 472-481.

[41] One rupee is equal to approximately 20 cents in U. S. Currency, or $1.00 in U. S. currency equals 5 rupees, written Rs. 5.

[42] Sidhwa, "The Training of Secondary Teachers in the State of Bombay," p. 13.

[43] H. N. Orange, Director General of Education in India, *Progress of Education in India, 1902-1907* (Fifth Quinquennial Review; Calcutta: Superintendent Government Printing, 1909), pp. 216-218.

and geography received the most stress among the literary subjects.[44]

Originally, Secondary Training College was under the jurisdiction of the Bombay State Government. A board comprised of members of the training college staff and inspectors from the Department of Public Instruction was charged with the evaluation of the candidates. This evaluation was based on the student's teaching ability and the results of examinations given throughout the year. Those students who successfully completed the one-year training program were awarded the Secondary Teacher's Certificate Diploma.[45,46]

With the establishment of a Secondary Teacher's Certificate Examination in 1899, and the Secondary Training College in 1906, the state's need for qualified[47] teachers was still far from being met. The shortage of qualified teachers was particularly acute in the privately managed secondary schools which, owing to the encouragement of state funds, had replaced the state schools as the dominant secondary institution in Bombay. This shortage in the private schools was aggravated by the state's policy of reserving only five of its thirty-five training college places for teachers from the non-government schools.[48]

Despite a central government resolution in 1913 stating that no teacher should be allowed to teach without a certificate,[49] and central grants from 1917 to 1922 for the expansion and improvement of education in the State of Bombay,[50] the Secondary Training College, which was the only institution for training secondary teachers in the state, did not increase its enrolment during this period. By 1921-22 only about one-fourth of the state's secondary teachers had

[44] Ibid., p. 216.

[45] Sidhwa, "The Training of Secondary Teachers in the State of Bombay," p. 18.

[46] K.S. Vakil, "The Secondary Training College, Bombay—A Retrospect." The Miscellany of the Secondary Training College : Bombay, Golden Jubilee Souvenir, 1906-1956, ed. N.R. Parasnis (Bombay 1956), p. 57.

[47] The term qualified refers to both those who successfully pass the Secondary Teacher's Certificate Examination and those who earn the Secondary Teacher's Certificate Diploma from the Secondary Training College. Only the latter group, however, are considered to be trained.

[48] Sidhwa, "The Training of Secondary Teachers in the State of Bombay," p. 35.

[49] Nurullah and Naik, A History of Education in India, p. 530.

[50] Naik, A Review of Education in Bombay State, p. 25.

either successfully completed the year's training program at the Secondary Training College or passed the Secondary Teacher's Certificate Examination.[51]

In addition to the problem of inadequate training facilities in terms of the required number of secondary teachers, charges were leveled against the low quality of students and the superficiality of the college's training program. These criticisms, generally applicable throughout India, were brought to the nation's attention in the "Report of the Calcutta University Commission, 1917-1919," commonly named the Sadler Report after the Commission's president, Sir Michael Sadler, Vice Chancellor of Leeds University in England. This report pointed to the need for the increased supply of trained teachers and also criticized the existent training program for its cramped syllabus and overemphasis on examinations.[52]

Although the commission restricted its study to Calcutta University, the Government of India endorsed the report in the belief that the findings had nationwide applicability.[53] After taking the report under consideration Bombay University officials agreed to affiliate the Secondary Training College, thereby placing the responsibility for secondary teacher training with the university and replacing the Secondary Teacher's Certificate Diploma with the Bachelor of Teaching Degree.[54]

The financial support of the central government met the cost to Bombay University for administering the Secondary Training College and also resulted in the increase of the Secondary Training College's yearly budget from Rs. 47,000 to Rs. 53,000.[55] This budget increase permitted the training college to add two lecturers and one assistant lecturer to the staff of a principal and vice-principal, and, in 1927, the student enrolment was increased from thirty-five to sixty.[56]

The curriculum for the Bachelor of Teaching degree (B.T.),

[51] Nurullah and Naik, *A History of Education in India*, p. 531.

[52] India, *Calcutta University Commission, 1917-19*, (Calcutta : Superintendent Government Printing, 1919), III, Part I, p. 211.

[53] Dongerkerry, *A History of the University of Bombay*, p. 74.

[54] *Handbook of the University of Bombay, 1922-23* (Bombay : Government Central Press), p. 61.

[55] *Report of the Director of Public Instruction in the Bombay Presidency, 1922-23*, (Bombay : Government Central Press, 1924), p. 40.

[56] Sidhwa, "The Training of Secondary Teachers in the State of Bombay," p. 19.

instituted in 1922-23, differed from the former diploma curriculum in two significant ways. First, since all of the B.T. candidates were required to be college graduates, the curriculum was restricted to education subjects. The prerequisite of a university degree would, it was assumed, insure adequate knowledge of the subject matter which the B. T. candidate would teach in the secondary school.

Second, the curriculum reflected some of the early twentieth century British advances in pedagogical theory and evidenced the beginning of a focus on India's particular educational problems.

The course of study as prescribed by the University was divided into three categories as follows :

1. Science of Education—philosophy and psychology. A study of the aims of education, the function of the school with regard to child development, the acquisition of skill, knowledge and tact, and the development of conduct, will and character.

2. History of Education—A study of the history of education in Europe from the Renaissance, a study of India's educational history, and present-day problems in education with special reference to the problems of India.

3. Practice of Education—A study of school management, including hygiene, the methods of teaching in general, and the methods of teaching particular subjects, at least one of which had to be either English or Science. The other options included classical languages, vernacular languages, mathematics, history and geography.[57]

Judging from the 1922 change in curriculum, the first major alteration in the training of secondary teachers since the founding of the Secondary Training College in 1906, the affiliation of the college to the university, augured a more progressive approach to teacher training. A survey of the annual handbooks of Bombay University, however, reveals the occurrence of only relatively minor curriculum changes during the first thirty years of the B.T. program. These included the addition of a course in experimental psychology and educational statistics and the deletion of the course in the history of European education. Also, the candidates were no longer required to offer English or science as one of their

[57] *Handbook of the University of Bombay, 1922-23,* p. 62.

teaching subjects, thus permitting complete freedom of choice of two special methods subjects.

In addition to these changes in the theoretical portion of the curriculum, the work in the practical portion of the curriculum was clearly enunciated during this period. The following degree requirements, which have remained in effect to the present, were instituted in 1929-30 :

1. Attendance at demonstration and discussion lessons.
2. Observation of teaching as directed.
3. Teaching practice of not less than 30 hours.
4. Attendance at tutorials for discussion of practice teaching.
5. Practical experience of educational psychology and experimental education.[58]

The university examination for the B.T. degree, which closely resembled the Secondary Teacher's Certificate Examination in form, consisted of a written examination on the theoretical portion of the curriculum and a practical examination in which the candidate was expected to demonstrate his skill in class management and teaching in both of his teaching subjects. In addition to this examination, the headmaster's evaluation of the candidate's practical work conducted throughout the year was considered in the process of making a judgment for awarding the degree.[59]

Advanced training in education beyond the B.T. degree was begun in 1936 when Bombay University instituted the Master of Education degree. The work for this degree consisted of two years of research on a thesis under the supervision of a guide appointed by the university.[60]

In 1941 the Ph. D. degree in education was instituted, and seven years later, the Indian Institute of Education was founded in Bombay for the purpose of training candidates for advanced degrees,[61] thus providing the required institutional framework for the advanced study of education as advocated in the Sadler Re-

[58] *Bombay University Handbook, 1929-30* (Bombay : Karnatak Press, 1929), p. 227.

[59] *Handbook of the University of Bombay, 1922-23*, pp. 61-62.

[60] *Handbook of the University of Bombay* (Bombay : Commercial Printing Press, 1937), Part II, pp. 214-215.

[61] Sidhwa, "The Training of Secondary Teachers in the State of Bombay," p. 28.

port.[62] Instead of functioning as a department or faculty of the university, however, the Institute operated independently for a period of approximately ten years, after which it ceased to function, primarily because of lack of funds.

The proposal to establish a department of education in Bombay University was first advanced in 1941.[63] The University's rejection of this proposal can, in part, be explained by the persistence of the view that the professional course for the preparation of teachers could be accomplished in the existing B.T. program and that further study should be academic rather than professional.[64] Others felt that graduate study could be carried out in the training college and therefore a university department of education was not necessary. Still a third argument held that the education faculty was not strong enough to qualify as a separate faculty. Regardless of the reason, the establishment of an education department did not have a sufficient priority on the claim for the necessary financial support, and, therefore, it did not come into being.

In 1927, the year in which the Secondary Training College's enrolment was raised from thirty-five to sixty, only twenty-two percent of the teachers in the State of Bombay's secondary schools were trained.[65] Furthermore, the Hartog Commission pointed out, Bombay was the only state in India which did not show an increase in the percentage of trained teachers in the five year period from 1922 to 1927.[66]

The enrolment of the Secondary Training College was increased to seventy-five in 1931, but this still did not meet the demand for trained teachers, and, even though the percentage of places for non-government teachers was raised,[67] the private schools, in particular, suffered from a shortage of trained teachers.[68]

[62] Calcutta University Commission, 1917-19, V, Part II, p. 71.

[63] Dongerkerry, History of the University of Bombay, p. 111.

[64] D.S. Gordon, The Training of Teachers in Indian Universities (Baroda, India : Inter-University Board, 1932), p. 2.

[65] Sidhwa, "The Training of Secondary Teachers in the State of Bombay," p. 29.

[66] India, Statutory Commission, Auxiliary Committee, Review of Growth of Education in British India : Interim Report of the Indian Statutory Commission, (Calcutta : Government of India Central Publication Branch, 1929), p. 115.

[67] The exact figures with respect to places for non-government teachers was not available.

[68] Naik, A Review of Education in Bombay State, p. 286.

In the main, the reason for the lag in the development of training colleges was due to their costly operation. Private enterprise
was reluctant to establish such colleges because of the great financial deficit in operation they were likely to incur. The low student-
teacher ratio (10 : 1) required in the training colleges as contrasted
to arts colleges, such as Elphinstone College or Wilson College,
was the chief cause of this relatively high operating cost. Neverthe-
less, Bombay State was able to add its second training college in
1934 at Kolhapur and a third the following year at Baroda.[69]

In 1944, the Central Advisory Board of Education prepared a
detailed report entitled, *The Post-War Educational Development in
India*, commonly known as the Sargent Report. The significance of
this document lies primarily in its recommendation that the secondary schools no longer be merely preparatory institutions for the
university. To remedy this deficiency, the Sargent Report recommended that in addition to the academic high schools, in which
the arts and pure sciences were taught, technical high schools be
established for imparting instruction in applied sciences such as
industrial, commercial and agricultural subjects.[70] This separation
of institutions at the secondary level extended to teacher training,
for the report expressed the view that no special training schools
were required for technical teachers, but, rather, they should
receive their instruction in technical institutions and receive practical experience in industry in order to qualify as teachers.[71]

While it may not be justifiable to say that the lack of a training
program for other than academic teachers was a result of the Sargent Report, nonetheless, the attitude expressed in this report pre-
vailed, and, as technical high schools developed under the auspices
of the central and state governments, pedagogical training for the
teachers in these institutions was not undertaken.

The advocacy of technical high schools in 1944 represented a
pre-independence effort to rectify the overemphasis on academic
subjects which had characterized Indian secondary education from
its beginnings. Although it was not felt that technical teachers
required pedagogical training, the espousal of the view that technical
instruction could profitably be carried out in an institutional,

[69] *Ibid.*, p. 272.
[70] Nurullah and Naik, *A History of Education in India*, 833-836.
[71] India, Central Advisory Board of Education, *Post-War Educational Development in India* (Sargent Report) (Delhi : Bureau of Education, 1944), p. 44.

post-primary setting, represented a first step toward the diversification of secondary education.

The decision to establish technical high schools was clearly the result of British influence; John Sargent, the Englishman after whom the report is named, obviously exerted a strong influence in his capacity as an educational advisor to the Indian Government. Nonetheless, throughout the history of British rule in India the power to make decisions relating to education followed an unwavering course in the direction of increased Indian *vis-a-vis* British control. In 1921 Indian jurisdiction over education was substantially increased when a system of political dyarchy was introduced, whereby central administration was divided into two parts; the "reserve" powers such as finance and police powers were continued under the control of the British Governor-General, but the "transferred" powers, including education, were given to Indian ministers.[72]

Dyarchy did not succeed in putting total control into Indian hands, for many Englishmen remained in key educational posts, and the control of finances remained with the British at both the state and central levels. British domination of education was finally brought to an end in 1937, however, when the system of dyarchy was replaced by the rule enunciated in the "Government of India Act of 1935", which granted complete autonomy to the states—in all but the areas of foreign relations, defence, ecclesiastical affairs and the administration of tribal areas.[73]

Under dyarchy and the "Government of India Act of 1935" the interest and support of the central government waned, and education increasingly became the province of the states. With the granting of complete independence to India in 1947, once again the central government renewed its interest and activities in education. Although the Constitution of 1950 relegated education's control to the states, the Indian government, under the domination of the prime minister and the Congress Party, wields considerable influence in what may be termed an "advisory" capacity.[74]

While primary education had the first claim to national funds, it was on secondary education, generally acknowledged to be

[72] Naik, *A Review of Education in Bombay State*, pp. 26-34.

[73] *Ibid.*

[74] Norman D. Palmer, *The Indian Political System*, (Boston : Houghton Mifflin Company, 1961), p. 96.

India's weak educational link under the British, that the greatest interest was focused and the most significant change contemplated.

As a corollary to the new nation's commitment to the creation of a democratic social order, the multipurpose high school was adopted as the accepted pattern of secondary education.[75] This institution, envisioned in the *Report of the Secondary Education Commission of 1953*, would ultimately provide the secondary education required for meaningful vocational and civic participation in the society to all citizens.

However, before the multipurpose high school could be established, teachers with an understanding and appreciation of this new design for secondary education had to be trained. Although the training colleges affiliated to Bombay University had become partially oriented to the Indian society by virtue of their control being placed in Indian hands and their curriculum being increasingly concerned with national educational problems, the secondary school was still primarily viewed as a preparation for the university, and the function of the training colleges was restricted to the training of academic subject matter teachers.

[75] N. S. Junankar, *Asian Review*, LVII, No. 216 (October, 1962), p. 236.

CHAPTER II

THE NEW AIMS OF INDIA'S SECONDARY TEACHER TRAINING

THE ISSUANCE of the *Report of the Secondary Education Commission* in September, 1953, hereafter referred to as the Mudaliar Report after the Commission chairman, A. Lakshmanaswami Mudaliar, marked a highly significant milepost in the development of Indian education in general, and especially its secondary education. In essence, this report represents independent India's educational prescription for a democratic, industrializing society.[1]

Subsequent to India's independence in 1947, secondary education came increasingly to the forefront of national attention. The need for technicians trained in the skills acquired at the secondary level, so vital to an industrializing society, and primary teachers, essential for the accomplishment of universal primary education, necessitated the expansion and reform of secondary education. To accomplish this, the foremost recommendation of the Mudaliar Commission was that the secondary system, geared almost exclusively to an academic program leading to the university, be replaced by a diversified system through the conversion of existing secondary schools and the creation of new secondary schools of a multipurpose nature.[2]

These multipurpose schools were intended to provide education of a terminal nature in addition to preparing students for university admission. Through an added emphasis on vocational and civic responsibilities, the instruction was to be diversified and made more functional in terms of the nation's economic and political requirements.

[1] *Report of the Secondary Education Commission*, pp. 1-2. The Commission, composed of nine members, seven Indians, one Englishman and one American, undertook its study of secondary education throughout India at the direction and under the sponsorship of the Indian Government.

[2] Margaret L. Cormack, *She Who Rides a Peacock*; (Bombay : Asia Publishing House, 1961), p. 35.

22

The curriculum, in the functional, comprehensive scheme of education, was to include core subjects taken in common by all students consisting of languages, general science, social studies and a craft. In addition, students were able to select a course of study from the following seven groups of diversified subjects : humanities, sciences, technical subjects, commercial subjects, agricultural subjects, fine arts and home sciences.[3-4] A further key feature of the multipurpose schools lay in the drastically altered methods of instruction which were to characterize them. Traditional practices, epitomized by virtually exclusive reliance on the lecture, were to give way to a more dynamic approach with a dual emphasis on the activity of the learner and practical work.[5]

From a political standpoint, the Mudaliar Report represents an effort on the part of the national government to strengthen its own influence on secondary education, at least to the point of prescribing the broad outline of an educational system consonant with the creation of a "Sovereign Democratic Republic."[6]

As previously noted in chapter one, subsequent to the granting of complete independence in 1947, the administration and control of education had become firmly established in the hands of the states, largely as a means of ensuring an optimal Indian voice in educational matters. Therefore, in order for the Mudaliar Report's recommendations to be implemented, either the central government's educational powers had to be formally expanded, or else the state's voluntary acceptance of central policy was necessary.

The Indian Constitution, adopted in 1950, fully acknowledged the right of the individual states to control education by relegating it to the State List, which contains those powers exercised solely by the states. The rationale for the central government's entering into the realm of education stems partially from the Constitution's Union List, which contains powers exercised exclusively by the

---

[3] *Mudaliar Report*, p. 188.

[4] Maharashtra State, Government of Maharashtra, Education and Social Welfare Department, *Education in Maharashtra, Annual Administration Report, 1959-60* (Nagpur, India : Government Press, 1963), p. 134. In the State of Maharashtra a multipurpose school is officially defined as one providing instruction in one or more of the seven groups of vocational subjects in addition to the usual group of academic subjects.

[5] *Mudaliar Report*, p. 91.

[6] M. R. Palande, *Introduction to the Indian Constitution* (6th ed. ; London : Oxford University Press, 1956), p. 154.

central government, and, to a greater extent, from the Concurrent List, which contains powers exercised jointly by the central government and the states. The former list is restricted to provisions for the training of various military personnel and the establishment of national libraries and scientific or technical institutions, while the Concurrent List includes vocational and technical training and professional training.

Although these central powers included on the Concurrent List might conceivably suggest possible controls over secondary education and, more especially, secondary teacher training, which could be considered professional training ; in practice, it has been the Constitution's welfare clause, authorizing the central government to enunciate "Directive Principles of State Policy", that has been used as the basis for the central government's activities in education.[7]

Rather than a legalistic approach, the central government has relied primarily on the voluntary cooperation of the states in educational matters. In order to ensure such cooperation, the former Minister of Education, M. C. Chagla, has advocated that education be placed on the Concurrent List,[8] but the prospects for such a constitutional revision appear problematical and, even if it were to come about, the acceptance by the states of any educational policy involving the expenditure of other than central funds would require a significant degree of voluntariness on the part of the states for its successful implementation.[9]

Since the states are free to reject the central government's funds and to ignore its advice, special bodies have been created to enlist the cooperation of the states. Chief among these is the University Grants Commission (UGC), which was appointed by the Indian Government in 1953. This body originally had the restricted task of dispensing funds to universities in order to encourage their development along scientific and technical lines. The role of this autonomous body has gradually expanded, however, to the point where it now plays a responsible role in the general area of standards and

[7] Kathryn G. Heath, *Ministries of Education : Their Functions and Organization*, (Washington : United States Government Printing Office, 1962), p. 330.

[8] *Times of India* (Bombay), March 9, 1964.

[9] For an extended discussion of central government-state relations see.... Selig Harrison, *India : The Most Dangerous Decades*, (Princeton : Princeton University Press, 1960) or Paul Appleby, *Public Administration in India : Report of a Survey*, (New Delhi : Government of India Press, 1957).

facilities in the nation's entire higher educational enterprise.[10] Although the munificence and influence of the UGC has not as yet extended to secondary teacher training, one of the commission's members called upon the principals of the training colleges to present a statement indicating their financial needs for inclusion in India's Fourth Five Year Plan commencing in 1966.[11]

At the secondary level the Central Advisory Board of Education (C. A. B. E.) and the All-India Council of Secondary Education (A. I. C. S. E.) have been formed to enlist the voluntary cooperation of the states. These bodies, composed of representatives of the states, do not have any constitutional authority, but, owing to their representative composition and willingness to compromise their individual positions in order to secure unanimous decisions, have been successful in establishing national policy aimed at reconstructing secondary education in the manner proposed by the Mudaliar Report.[12] In 1955 the C. A. B. E. unanimously concluded that :

"(1) The end of secondary education at seventeen plus should mark a terminal stage in education and prepare students for life. (2) It should also be of a standard which would enable them to participate with profit in the three years' degree course."[13]

The pronouncement by the board established a nationally agreed-upon age for leaving secondary school, thus achieving a degree of national uniformity, and, more important for our purposes, it signified an acceptance on the part of the states of the multipurpose pattern of secondary education.

Although the states have, at least tacitly, accepted the central government's plan for the reconstruction of secondary education, albeit through a representative body, progress towards the establishment of multipurpose schools has been very slow. One of the chief obstacles is the solid entrenchment of the existing type of

[10] United States Educational Foundation in India, *Handbook of Indian Universities* (New Delhi : Allied Publishers, 1963), pp. 8-9.

[11] J. G. Joshi, in address delivered at All India Principals of Training Colleges Conference, Mysore, India, June 10, 1964.

[12] India, Ministry of Education, *Reconstruction of Secondary Education* (New Delhi : Government of India, 1962), Preface.

[13] Humayun Kabir, *Education in New India* (London : George Allen and Unwin, 1956), pp. 64-69.

secondary education and secondary teacher training and the resultant difficulties involved in bringing about any change in the status quo. Throughout the history of the development of secondary teacher training, change, when it has occurred, has been of an evolutionary nature, resulting in only minor variations from the basic pattern prescribed at the outset of the establishment of the British system in India.

An examination of the operational context of secondary education and secondary teacher training in Maharashtra,[14] and the city of Bombay in particular, will not only reveal the slight extent to which multipurpose education has been established in the decade since the issuance of the Mudaliar Report, but it will also illustrate the inherent difficulties in accomplishing such a drastic transformation as that which has been proposed.

Unlike primary education, which is financed and controlled locally, and university education, which operates relatively free of state control, secondary education is largely regulated, supervised and financed by the state. The pattern of education in Western Maharashtra, the region in which Bombay is included, consists of four levels as indicated in Table 1.

At the primary stage, which is administered by the Bombay municipality, education is free, but only the first four standards (grades) are compulsory. Secondary education, comprising both the middle stage and the high school stage, is neither compulsory nor free.[15]

TABLE 1

PATTERN OF EDUCATION IN WEST MAHARASHTRA AND BOMBAY[16]

Level Designation	Years Included		Age
Lower Primary Stage	Standards	I-IV	6- 9
Full Primary Stage	Standards	I-VII	6-12
Middle Stage	Standards	V-VII	10-12
High School Stage	Standards	VIII-XI	13-16

[14] Norman D. Palmer, *The Indian Political System*, p. 139. In 1960, Bombay State was divided along linguistic lines into Maharashtra and Gujarat. The city of Bombay became the capital of Maharashtra.

[15] For our purposes secondary education is restricted to the high school stage. It will be noted in Table 1 that, although the middle stage is officially considered to be a part of secondary education, it does not go beyond the full primary stage. Teacher training for high school teachers is separate and distinct from that of middle school teachers.

[16] *Education in Maharashtra, Annual Administration Report, 1959-60*, p. 2.

The high schools in Bombay fall into four categories: the ordinary or academic high school, the technical high school, the vocational high school, and the multipurpose high school. As of the academic year 1963-64, the city of Bombay's total number of secondary institutions in each of these categories was as follows:[17-18]

Academic	440
Technical	22
Vocational	11
Multipurpose	33
Total	506

The technical high schools are administered by the State Director of Technical Instruction, a separate agency from the State Department of Public Instruction which has jurisdiction over all of the other secondary schools in Bombay.

With the exception of six of the technical high schools which are run directly by the state, the management of Bombay's high schools is in the hands of private governing bodies, legally termed societies.[19] These societies organize secondary schools, extract fees from the students for their operation and contribute from their own funds for the operation of their schools. To a very large extent, however, they rely on state funds, which amount to 45 percent of admissible expenditures in urban areas such as Bombay and 50 percent in rural areas, (See Table 2).

TABLE 2

SOURCES OF SECONDARY EDUCATION FUNDS IN MAHARASHTRA[20]

Source	Per cent of Total
State Government	51·3%
Student Fees	38·6%
Private Managing Body	9·5%
Other	·6%[a]

[a]The remaining .6% includes limited central government contributions, allocated to schools which impart technical instruction, and municipal or district contributions.

[17] Maharashtra State, Directorate of Education, *Letter No. P. 14-R164* (Poona, India: May 12, 1964).

[18] Mimeographed list in office of M. Y. Bhide, Deputy Director of Technical Education, State of Maharashtra, undated but current as of May, 1964.

[19] India, *The Societies Registration Act, 1860* (as modified up to January 1, 1963), (New Delhi : Government of India Press, 1963).

[20] *Education in Maharashtra, Annual Administration Report, 1959-60*, p. 120. These figures are for the entire State of Maharashtra, but are representative of Bombay.

The state is able to exercise considerable control over these privately operated secondary institutions by means of its power of recognition, a prerequisite to gaining state funds, as set forth in *The Code for Recognition of and Grant-in-Aid to Secondary Schools*.[21] The nature and extent of the state's control is clearly illustrated by the conditions required for recognition contained in the code. For example, there must be a definite need for the school in the locality in which it is to be situated, so that there will not be any competition with existing institutions. The management of the proposed school must be adjudged to be competent, and the school's financial stability must be assured. Also, the physical plant must meet the code's requirements with respect to safety and sanitation.

The state's jurisdiction over secondary education extends to the administration and educational program of the schools as well as the conditions for the initial establishment of an institution. In order to be recognized by the state the school must charge approved fees, pay salaries in accordance with a state-wide pay scale, and maintain records prescribed by the state. The curriculum and textbook selections are laid down by the state, as are the standards for promotion from one grade to the next. The Department of Public Institutions enforces these requirements by means of periodic inspection by members of its staff.[22]

Owing to the controls on secondary education exercised by the state and the dependence of the high schools on state funds, the conversion of existing secondary schools to multipurpose institutions would clearly require initiative at the state level.

As the number of each type of secondary institution attests, the academic high school continues to be the predominant secondary institution in Bombay. Insofar as they provide other than academic instruction, the vocational and technical high schools bear certain resemblances to multipurpose education. The vocational high schools offer one or more of the diversified multipurpose courses without a course of academic subjects and are terminal institutions.[23] The technical high schools even more closely approximate the multipurpose school, for they offer an academic curriculum consisting of three languages (mother tongue, Hindi, and English),

[21] *The Code for Recognition and Grant-in-Aid to Secondary Schools* (Bombay: Government of Maharashtra Education and Social Welfare Department, 1963).

[22] *Ibid.*, p. 5.

[23] *Education in Maharashtra, Annual Administration Report, 1959-60*, p. 135.

mathematics and science, in addition to machine drawing, workshop technology and electrical and mechanical engineering.[24] Further-more, these institutions prepare graduates for further study of a techni-cal or scientific nature in either a diploma course in institutions called polytechnics or a Bachelor of Science program in the university. In addition, the training could be considered terminal as the graduates of technical high schools are capable of securing employ-ment utilising the skills that they have acquired in their training.[25]

Although vocational and technical high schools bear a resem-blance to the multipurpose high school, they do not necessarily constitute a practical step in the direction of the establishment of multipurpose institutions, but, rather, represent an alternative to the multipurpose school. Nor is the multipurpose school as estab-lished as its numbers would seem to suggest. With one noteworthy exception,[26] Bombay's multipurpose high schools operate as separate technical and academic high schools.

Entrance requirements differ, depending on whether one wishes to be accepted for the technical or academic curriculum, and, once admitted, the students are segregated according to the curriculum they pursue. In one institution this dichotomy is carried to the extreme of having two separate buildings on opposite sides of the road. The only commonly shared feature of this institution was its headmaster, who made no secret of the fact that the multipurpose designation of his institution was for the expedient purpose of securing funds from the central government for the construction of the technical division of his "multipurpose" high school.[27]

Many factors must be considered in an attempt to account for the lack of success in establishing multipurpose education in Bombay to date. These can perhaps be summarized as lack of adequate

[24] Interview with principal, multipurpose high school, Bombay, March 11, 1964.

[25] India, Ministry of Scientific Research and Cultural Affairs, *Technical Education in India Today*, by L. S. Chandrikah (New Delhi: Government of India, 1963), p. 10.

[26] This exceptional institution, the Amulakh Amichand B. V. Vidyaylaya Multipurpose High School, probably corresponds most nearly to the multipurpose high school envisioned in the Mudaliar Report of all such institutions in India. The principal of this school, Soli Pavri, has been influenced by his personal observations of high schools in the United States.

[27] Interview with principal, multipurpose high school, March 11, 1964. This institution qualifies under the Maharashtra definition of a multipurpose high school, i.e., one containing both an academic and at least one of the diversified curricula.

finances, lack of demand and insufficient understanding of the concept of multipurpose education.

The central government and the State of Maharashtra combined can do little more than meet approximately one-half of the cost of the multipurpose school. The societies are understandably reluctant to establish other than academic high schools, as the burden of costs not met by either the central government or the state would devolve upon them. The societies, in turn, would invariably pass on to the students the increased educational costs in the form of higher tuition fees. The deleterious result of these increased costs would be that the multipurpose schools would become even more economically and socially exclusive than the secondary schools are at present.

Much of the above reasoning regarding finances is moot in any case. The population at large and the societies in particular consider the pursuit of academic subjects the necessary means for attaining a coveted place in the university and an ultimate position of social and economic standing in the society. Hence, they are extremely wary of any institution that is not a tried and proven avenue to university entrance and, in particular, one which openly professes goals other than preparation for admission to the university.

Given the entrenched position of secondary institution other than the multipurpose type and the lack of demand and finances for this institution, its eventual establishment on a mass scale is clearly an uncertainty. Nonetheless, the most basic requirement for the successful establishment of multipurpose schools is the personnel capable of educating both prospective teachers and the public with regard to the need and benefits, both personal and social, to be derived from such an institution. The most logical repository for this task would seem to be the institutions concerned with the training of secondary teachers; namely the secondary teacher training colleges.

It is axiomatic that even the beginnings of multipurpose education require teachers who have acquired the knowledge of the academic and diversified curricula and the necessary skills for teaching in the setting appropriate to these institutions. Such knowledge and skills must first, of course, be possessed by those engaged in the training of such teachers.

In any analysis of an institution's progress towards specific goals or prospects for such progress, it is first essential to acquire an understanding of the administrative context in which the institution operates. In the case of the secondary training colleges the control and influence of the state and the university and the present alternatives to the training colleges must be examined, for only when seen in relationship to the external agencies of control and the total context of teacher training can the efforts of the training colleges to train multipurpose teachers be appraised.

Although the task of training secondary teachers has to a great extent been delegated to the university, the extent to which the state continues to exercise its responsibility in the teacher training domain is evidenced by the manner in which it undertakes to compensate for the university's limitations, both in terms of quantity and subject matter diversity of teachers. The insufficient quantity of trained teachers is partially compensated for by a State Secondary Teachers' Certificate Examination, and the inability of the university to train other than subject-matter teachers is, in part, met through special state-affiliated training institutions.

The Secondary Teachers' Certificate Examination (S.T.C.E.), conducted by a committee appointed by the State Director of Education, is open to candidates at least 17 years of age who have passed the Secondary School Certificate Examination. In addition, these candidates must have at least 9 months of teaching experience in a secondary school, or Standards V-VII in a primary school, or have undergone the prescribed course of instruction at an examination institute recognized by the state. One part of the examination consists of a lesson which is assessed by a representative of the Department of Public Instruction. In addition, there is a theoretical portion of the examination which is administered by the principal of the Government Secondary Training College.[28]

Since 1953 the number taking this Examination in Maharashtra has increased from approximately 400 to 8,000 students. Approximately 25 per cent or 2,000 of these are from Bombay.[29] The major impetus for this increase was the ruling in 1953 that candidates could take the examination in Gujarati, Marathi, Hindi or English instead of exclusively in English as was formerly the case.[30]

The increasing popularity of the examination has led to the

[28] *Rules for the Secondary Teachers Certificate Examination* (Poona, India : Yerauda Prison Press, 1958), p. 1.

[29] Interview with N. R. Parasnis, Principal, Secondary Training College, Bombay, May 25, 1964.

[30] *Rules for the Secondary Teachers Certificate Examination*, p. 4.

establishment of Secondary Teachers Certificate Institutions designed solely for the preparation of candidates for the examination. In the Bombay region there are 76 such institutions, training over 1,000 candidates. The fact that these institutions offer this instruction in the evenings, thus enabling the students (and faculty) to teach or to be otherwise gainfully employed during the day, further helps to account for the popularity of the examination as a means of becoming a qualified teacher.

Although they are considered trained secondary teachers, those who successfully pass the examination are not on a par with Bachelor of Education graduates who are college graduates. Normally, they are employed in the middle schools, while Bachelor of Education graduates are employed in the high schools.

The training colleges affiliated to the university restrict their training to academic subject-matter teachers, while the high school has a considerably broader curriculum.[31] The state, therefore, makes the necessary provisions to insure a supply of qualified teachers in the non-academic areas. By way of illustration, art teachers are trained in the J. J. School of Art in Bombay which maintains a department of teacher training and prepares candidates for the State Drawing Teachers Examination.[32] Physical education teachers receive their training in institutions created for that express purpose. Graduates qualify for a diploma in Physical Education at Kandivali, while high school graduates may qualify for certificates in any of eleven institutions throughout the state.[33]

The teachers of technical subjects offered in either the technical or multipurpose high schools, who come under the jurisdiction of the State Director of Technical Education, for the most part do not receive any pedgogical training. However, the view that technical teachers do not require such training is being increasingly questioned.

In 1959, the central government financed pioneering efforts in the training of technical teachers at the Central Training Institute at Chembur, a suburb of Bombay. This institution awards the Instructor of Skilled Workers' Certificate for successful completion of a nine-months period of training.[34]

[31] Appendix II, Primary and Secondary Academic Curriculum in Bombay.
[32] *Education in Maharashtra, Annual Administration Report, 1959-60*, p. 187.
[33] *Ibid.*, pp. 252-253.
[34] Interview with A.G. Ghaisas, Elphinstone Technical High School, Bombay, February 18, 1964.

Essentially, the state has delegated the task of training secondary teachers to the university. It was felt that the affiliation of Secondary Training College to Bombay University would result in attracting more highly qualified individuals to secondary teaching and would provide an improved training program. The university was providing a service to the state by overseeing the training of teachers, to be sure, but, by restricting the training under its auspices to that of academic subject-matter teachers, it evidenced a concern for the continued domination of the academic secondary school and, indirectly, its own self-enhancement.

Although the university grants the degrees, the actual instruction takes place in the three training colleges affiliated to the university. The university exercises its direct control over the training colleges through the Board of Studies. This board is responsible for the curriculum, the prescription of textbooks, and the degree examination. For the Master of Education and the Ph. D. in Education degrees it approves the topics for theses and dissertations and appoints referees for evaluating them. Also, it prescribes the criteria for students' admission and appointment of faculty members.

The representation of training college personnel on the fourteen member Board suggests considerable self-government on the part of the training colleges. Each of the three training colleges is represented by the department heads of their psychology; history and administration departments, respectively. In addition to these nine members, two faculty representatives are chosen from the colleges at large. The remaining three members are co-opted from outside the university. The chairman is elected from among the Board members, and at present, is one of the co-opted members, a headmaster of one of Bombay's foremost academic secondary schools.

The training colleges, however, do not enjoy the autonomy that the composition and purview of the Board of Studies would suggest. Rather, it represents the lowest link in the university's chain of command. Any higher body has a veto power on the Board of Studies' decisions, and broad policy decisions are reserved to these higher bodies. First, the decisions of the board must go to the Academic Council which consists of all the chairmen of the Boards of Studies for the various disciplines and the heads of all of the colleges affiliated to the university.

Upon approval by the Academic Councils, the original decisions of the board go to the Syndicate for its final approval. The

Syndicate is the university's executive authority in both administrative and academic matters and is composed of representatives of the state government.[35]

The highest governing body of the university is the Senate. Changes in major policy matters and the university constitution are subject to its approval. Some of its members are nominated by the Chancellor, the titular head of the university; the rest are elected by university and college teachers, headmasters, selected alumni, representatives of local economic and civic bodies, state legislators and major donors.

With the passage of the Bombay University Act of 1953, the university's jurisdiction was restricted to the greater Bombay area.[36] As a result, the university is increasingly gearing its curriculum to the study of urban problems. Such an orientation would appear to be in harmony with the concept of multipurpose education; however, the revisions required on the part of the university in order for the training colleges to assume the task of training multipurpose teachers, go beyond curriculum additions and alterations.

In order for the training colleges to become multipurpose training institutions, the university would have to take one of the following three theoretical courses of action :

1. Broaden the Bachelor's degree programs so as to include training in the diversified multipurpose curricula.
2. Alter the present requirement that all Bachelor of Education candidates have a Bachelor's degree in order to include teachers of the non-academic curricula.
3. Devise a special program whereby teachers in the non-academic areas could be admitted into training colleges, although ineligible for the Bachelor of Education degree.

The university, a conservative body as attested to by the brief description of its administrative hierarchy, with largely a conservative mission—that of establishing and maintaining creditable academic standards—could hardly be considered a likely prime mover in the development of a type of secondary education other than that which would enhance its own standards.

---

[35] *Handbook of the University of Bombay (Part II)*, p. 33.
[36] As more colleges became established in the areas formerly under Bombay University's jurisdiction new universities were created to administer them.

The state's position with respect to the promotion of the training of multipurpose teachers is an ambivalent one. Just as the state supports a variety of secondary institutions, it also supports a variety of forms of secondary teacher training. Assuming that the training of multipurpose high school teachers should take place under one roof, or failing this, at least should consist of common training elements for all teachers, it is difficult to reconcile the state's simultaneous support of multipurpose education and institutions that are antithetical to multipurpose education.

Viewing the secondary training colleges from the perspective of their administrative context and their historical background, the likelihood that these institutions can or will adapt to the central government's scheme for multipurpose secondary education does not appear very great.

CHAPTER III

THE REFORMS IN BOMBAY UNIVERSITY'S SECONDARY TRAINING COLLEGES, 1953-54—1963-64

THE CONVERSION of secondary education from the traditional to the multipurpose pattern required certain changes in the training of the secondary teacher. In general, the curriculum of the secondary training colleges had to be broadened so as to include the preparation of teachers in the non-academic areas, and the training program had to adopt methods appropriate to this more diversified and practical curriculum.[1] Fortunately for our purposes, the Mudaliar Report addresses itself specifically to the training colleges and suggests directions which they might take in order to train the teachers required to staff schools of a multipurpose nature. As with the previous national educational reports, the recommendations of the Mudaliar Report are clearly applicable to Bombay.[2]

In tracing the efforts of Bombay University's training colleges to institute the reforms proposed by the Mudaliar Commission, four relatively distinct categories have been delineated. These are :

1. Broadening of the curriculum.
2. Use of less formal and more diverse methods.
3. Improvement of the quality of instruction.
4. Development of in-service education.

Although these particular categories are not explicitly outlined in the report, all of the proposals for secondary teacher training in the report can be subsumed under one of these headings.

In 1956 the curriculum for the training of secondary teachers

[1] *Secondary Teacher Training* (Paris : UNESCO. International Bureau of Education, 1954), pp. 99-100.

[2] *Mudaliar Report*, p. 1. The presence of two Bombay educators on the nine-man commission, J. A. Taraporevala and M. T. Vyas, serves to reenforce the credibility of this argument.

affiliated to Bombay University underwent its most far-reaching change. As with the curriculum change of 1922-23, which was prompted by the Sadler Report of 1919, the revision of 1956 was to a large extent the result of the recommendations of a national report; namely, the Mudaliar Report of 1953. The title of the program or the degree, which in 1922 was changed from Secondary Teacher's Certificate Diploma to the Bachelor of Training degree, was once again changed; this time to its present designation, the Bachelor of Education (B. Ed.) degree. The present name, it was felt, connoted greater academic prestige and is suggestive of the optimism with which the new curriculum was introduced.

Although the dual approach to training, through a separate theoretical and practical portion was retained with the curriculum change of 1956, and the major portion of the theoretical content underwent only a slight change, when the additions to the curriculum are taken into account, the significance of this revision becomes apparent.

Two major groups of courses were added to the curriculum. The first, indicated in Table 3 below, consists of five additions to the special method courses, which would in effect provide the training required for the teaching of the diversified subjects in the multipurpose curriculum.

TABLE 3

BOMBAY UNIVERSITY BACHELOR OF EDUCATION
SPECIAL METHODS COURSES[3]

(Candidates must take (any) two of the following)	
Inclusions Prior to 1956	*1956 Additions*
English	Technical Subjects
Modern Indian Languages	Commercial Subjects
Marathi, Hindi, Gujarati	Home Science
Sanskrit	Agriculture
Persian	Indian Administration and Civics
French	(or candidates may take any one of
History	the following crafts : Cardboard
Geography	Work and Book Binding, Leather
Mathematics	Work, Cane and Bamboo Work,
Science	Needle Work)

[3] *St. Xavier's Institute of Education Handbook* (Bombay : William Printing Press, 1962-63), p. 43.

The second major set of additions to the B. Ed. curriculum is termed the Special Fields of Education. Each student is required to take one course from among the following six special fields :[4]

1. Educational and Vocational Guidance.
2. Child Guidance.
3. Social Education.
4. History of Education in India . . . Ancient, Medieval and Modern up to 1854.
5. Education of the Handicapped.
6. Basic Education.

In general, the effect of these two groups of additions, the special methods subjects and the special fields of education, can be seen to be in keeping with the broad aims of providing a more functional and democratic secondary education as envisioned by the Mudaliar Report. While the special methods additions constitute a response to societal needs of an economic and political nature, the special fields of education are more closely oriented to the special needs and problems which individuals are likely to encounter in the context of a transforming social order.

With the addition of the diversified subjects to the special methods options the crucial question of whether or not teachers of these subjects required pedagogical training and, if so, where this training would most appropriately take place, apparently was finally resolved. Bombay's addition of these subjects was a direct response to the Mudaliar Report's suggestion that "teachers of technical and technological subjects . . . in the majority of cases be [university] graduates in the particular subject and should have received training in teaching it."[5] Presumably, prospective teachers in those areas not included in the university curriculum would nonetheless receive pedagogical training in the regular training colleges, after attaining the desired level of knowledge in their field at an appropriate state-approved institution.

This same suggestion was first advanced in the Abbot-Wood Report of 1937 which advocated that the "training colleges . . . be utilized in imparting to technical teachers pedagogic knowledge and

[4] *Ibid.*, p. 59.
[5] *Mudaliar Report*, p. 127.

skill,"[6] but it was not implemented by Bombay's Secondary Training College. Perhaps, owing to the difficulties involved in the implementation of the Abbot-Wood Report recommendations, the Sargent Report of 1944 recommended that the teachers of technical and commercial subjects receive practical experience in industry and pedagogical training in the technical institutions rather than the training colleges.[7]

In practice, prior to 1956 teachers of technical and vocational subjects did not receive any teacher training.[8] Apparently, the general assumption was that owing to the practical nature of these subjects, instruction in them alone would provide, by precept, the required knowledge and skills for teaching purposes. By way of illustration of this viewpoint, the principal of a multipurpose high school offering instruction in the technical subjects explained that his faculty, typically, had studied for four years beyond high school and held diplomas in mechanical or electrical engineering. When asked by a faculty member from one of the training colleges whether the fact that his faculty had not received teacher training hampered them in teaching, his response was, "No, it does not hamper their day to day work. They know nothing of psychology but they continue to teach according to methods by which they were taught." The training college faculty member, obviously dismayed by this response, then inquired whether these teachers were less loyal to the teaching profession. To this the principal replied, "Perhaps—it is not evident in their teaching, but they may leave after a few years."[9]

In any event the traditional deep-seated dichotomy of humanistic and technical studies which pervades all Indian education was not to be countermanded by the formality of adding diversified subjects to the B. Ed. curriculum. As the chairman of Bombay University's Board of Studies of Education indicated, the addition of these subjects meant only that they, potentially, could be offered.[10]

[6] A. Abbott and S.H. Wood, *Report on Vocational Education in India With a Section on General Education and Administration* (Place of publication not given, 1937), p. 104.

[7] *Post-War Educational Development in India*, p. 64.

[8] See Appendix III, The High School Curriculum proposed by the Mudaliar Commission for a listing of technical subjects and other diversified subjects to be offered in the multipurpose high schools.

[9] Interview with principal, Multipurpose High School, March 11, 1964.

[10] Interview with A. S. Sthalekar, Chairman, Board of Studies of Education, Bombay University, May 7, 1964.

In fact, their addition was academic ; they have not been offered, nor is it likely that they will be offered in the near future.

In 1958 the central government renewed its efforts to persuade the training colleges to train teachers in the non-academic areas. The All India Council for Secondary Education (A.I.C.S.E.) formally requested the training colleges to train teachers in the diversified subjects as a part of the regular B. Ed. program. In the case of diploma holders, e.g., non-university graduates, it was suggested that the training colleges organize special courses leading to a diploma in the teaching of their practical subject, rather than the B. Ed. degree.[11] This suggestion marked a compromise, whereby the training colleges would offer a program consisting of training in the practical subjects but would not afford to its graduates the status of the B. Ed. degree.

In response to the A. I. C. S. E.'s request, Bombay University's Secondary Training Colleges (S. T. C.) instituted special short-term courses of approximately four months duration in order to train teachers for the multipurpose high schools.[12] These were conducted for two years (1958-59, 1959-60) in two of the practical subjects, home science and commercial subjects, before being discontinued.[13]

From an official point of view the chief obstacle to training in the diversified subjects for prospective teachers is the absence of qualified faculty members.

Except in the case of teachers of commercial subjects, it is not possible to include training of teachers teaching the various diversified courses in multipurpose schools in the regular Bachelor of Education program as it is not possible to get graduates to teach technical subjects or Fine Arts and even Home Science.[14]

The usual explanation for the inability of the training colleges to secure qualified faculty members is that an individual with the required training and skills can command a much higher salary in

[11] *Reconstruction of Secondary Education*, p. 3.

[12] *Education in Maharashtra, Annual Administration Report, 1959-60*, p. 36.

[13] Interview with N. R. Parasnis, principal, Secondary Training College, May, 25, 1964.

[14] India, Ministry of Education, "Training of Teachers of Multipurpose Schools and Higher Secondary Schools (Government of Bombay)," *Proceedings of the Twenty-Sixth Meeting of the Central Advisory Board of Education* (New Delhi : Government of India Press, 1959, Appendix H (a).

business or industry. Another important consideration is the lack of demand for such courses. This is primarily owing to the same reason, namely, the attraction of more profitable occupations than teaching for those with technical backgrounds.

Since the discontinuance of the short-term courses in 1960, S.T.C. has not renewed its efforts to train teachers in the diversified subjects. St. Xavier's and Sadhana, the other training colleges affiliated to Bombay University, have likewise not offered such training, although the 1956 special methods additions continue to exist on paper. Hence, the most fundamental task in the creation of multi-purpose schools, the training of teachers in the non-academic or practical subjects has not been accomplished by Bombay University's training colleges.

The training colleges have met with success, however, in implementing the second major 1956 curriculum additions, the special fields of eduction. Every B. Ed. candidate is required to take one of these subjects.[15] These special fields additions stem directly from the Mudaliar recommendations and represent a vital part of the training of a multipurpose teacher. For example, in the case of guidance, the report reasons that regardless of what subject one may teach, "the provision of diversified courses of instruction imposes on teachers . . . the additional responsibility of giving proper guidance to pupils in their choice of courses and careers."[16]

The state of Maharashtra has played an active role in encouraging the training of guidance personnel. It became one of the first states to establish a state guidance service with the formation of the Institute for Vocational Guidance in 1950.[17] This Institute was largely responsible for the introduction of educational and vocational guidance both in the B. Ed. and the Master of Education (M. Ed) programs.[18]

At the B. Ed. level the guidance program is designed to equip the students to give career information and conduct group guidance, while instruction in the administering of tests and techniques of individual guidance is reserved for the M. Ed. students. The B.Ed.

[15] *St. Xavier's Handbook*, p. 59.

[16] *Mudaliar Report*, p. 107.

[17] John G. Odgers, *State Bureau of Educational and Vocational Guidance* (Delhi : Kapur Printing Press, 1962), p. 2.

[18] Interview with Miss J. Mascarenhas, faculty member, St. Xavier's, April 2, 1964.

course consists of a consideration of the nature of guidance, a survey of the various methods of evaluation ; including tests, interviews, questionnaires and cumulative records, and a survey of educational and occupational opportunities.[19]

In its statement on the aims and objectives for secondary education, the Mudaliar Report stresses the need for improving the nation's productive efficiency as a means toward the broader ultimate goal of a secular, democratic republic.[20] This, in turn, it is pointed out, calls for a view of education that transcends a narrow, academic approach[21] and relates the curriculum to community life.[22] Two Indian educational developments that embrace these ideals at the primary and adult levels, basic and social education, respectively, have been introduced into the B. Ed. curriculum as special fields subjects. These electives are felt to be of value to the prospective secondary teacher for insight into the conception of the relationship between education and social needs that they can provide.

Another reason for studying basic education is that it will contribute to the present Indian efforts at integrating secondary education with primary education as opposed to secondary education's present predominant orientation to university requirements. The basic education curriculum is studied solely for familiarization purposes. This curriculum stresses the child's physical and social environment. The child learns a craft such as weaving or woodworking as a means for preparing him for life in his particular environment. Although literary and arithmetical skills are included in the basic schools, the major emphasis is placed on activity as a means to learning.

Social education, or adult education, represents a manifestation of the interest and concern for the welfare of the community which educators are increasingly coming to express. Its foremost goal is the eradication of illiteracy, but, since its inception, its scope has been broadened to include child care, arts and crafts, and agriculture. The emphasis in this special fields course is on the underlying rationale and description of the social education programs, and it is not intended to prepare the secondary teacher for working with adults.

[19] *St. Xavier's Handbook*, p. 59.
[20] *Mudaliar Report*, p. 19.
[21] *Ibid.*, p. 20.
[22] *Ibid.*, p. 66.

While the study of guidance places the desired emphasis on the needs of the individual and demonstrates how education is a preparation for life, the study of social and basic education can be seen as emphasizing the community and the means by which education can have a direct bearing on the community's task of social and economic betterment. There remains a third focus ; the nation. In this connection the Mudaliar Report stipulates that secondary education should "equip its students adequately with civic as well as vocational efficiency—and the quality of character that goes with it so that they may be able to play their part worthily and completely in the improvement of national life."[23] The Bombay University 1956 curriculum revision for the B. Ed. program reflects this demand for heightened emphasis on civics in two specific instances. The study of the History of Education up to 1854 has been made optional in order to place greater concentration on the role of education in present day India. Second, a section entitled Education for Democracy with special reference to India's Constitution has been added to the philosophical portion of the theoretical curriculum.[24]

Incorporating the special fields of education into the curriculum did not present any particular difficulties to the training colleges, as was the case with the special methods diversified subjects. Regular faculty members were assigned to teach these subjects, and they were apparently able to familiarize themselves with the material in the syllabus for instructional purposes. With the exception of the teachers of guidance courses, who undertook special preparation through Bombay's Institute for Vocational Guidance, and the one faculty member, who had done a study of basic education in connection with his Ph. D. dissertation, there were no other evidences of specific preparation for instructing the special fields of education courses.

This expansion of the curriculum represents a beginning for the training colleges in the task of preparing multipurpose teachers. Although training for teachers in the non-academic subjects has not been instituted, through the introduction of the special fields of education and the increased emphasis on civics in the theoretical portion of the curriculum, the prospective teacher is at least being introduced to the broadened view of education's role envisaged by the Mudaliar Report.

[23] *Mudaliar Report,* p. 24.
[24] *St. Xavier's Handbook,* p. 46.

With respect to methods, the second category of change to be examined, the same unfortunate "stress on examinations and over-crowded syllabus"[25] which the Mudaliar Commission found in India's secondary schools, is also to be found in the training colleges. These ubiquitous features can simultaneously be assigned as causes for the pedantic methods employed in Indian post-primary education, and obstacles to any kind of reform. As the objectives of education are extended beyond the emphasis on symbols of academic achievement to include "love of work, clear thinking, and expansion of students' interests,"[26] the three major objectives of secondary education outlined in the Mudaliar Report, the responsibility for the development of these attributes in the teachers themselves naturally devolves upon the training colleges. The presupposition made here is that the methods used in the training of multipurpose teachers should provide a model for the instruction to be imparted in the secondary school. Methods reforms on the part of secondary teachers are ultimately dependent upon reforms in the training colleges.

It is extremely difficult to measure the extent to which the training colleges have reformed with respect to methods. The investigator, whose observations are limited to a single period of time, lacks the necessary knowledge of previous conditions needed for making comparisons. Written evidence of an analytical nature is virtually non-existent. Should one accept statements prepared for foreign consumption depicting a "richer, informal academic and social life,"[27] or can one assume from the tenor of much of the present Indian self-criticism that the "narrowness, verbalism and lifelessness reflected in the spirit and work of the training colleges"[28] persists to the present day?

In general, the present day observations of Indian and foreign observers alike differ little in kind from the findings made a decade ago by the Mudaliar Commission. In fact, much of the negative criticism today, particularly that of the Indians, is even more intense. While this suggests worsening conditions, it could also be

[25] *Mudaliar Report*, p. 17.
[26] *Ibid.*, pp. 84-87.
[27] Sureschandra Shukla, "The Education and Training of Teachers," *The Yearbook of Education, 1963*, eds. George Z. F. Bereday and Joseph A. Lauwerys (London : Evans Brothers, 1963), p. 336.
[28] K. L. Shrimali, *Better Teacher Education*, (New Delhi : Ministry of Education, Government of India, 1954), p. 23.

viewed as a favorable sign inasmuch as it denotes a more keenly felt awareness of the problems and a willingness to discuss them frankly, but in either case it does not afford reliable evidence with which to measure change.

The best single indication of methods' reforms in the training colleges is probably the testimony of the faculty of the training colleges, for it is the sole available criterion that has the necessary feature of perspective over a period of time. This information was obtained in a personal interview in which twenty-four of the three training colleges' twenty-six faculty members participated.[29]

When asked, "What do you consider to be the most significant change in the training colleges in the past ten years?" 62·5 per cent (fifteen of twenty-four) of the faculty respondents from Bombay University's three training colleges felt that change in the methods used in and advocated by the training colleges was of utmost significance. Although the rationale for this response varied, all of the fifteen felt that a greater degree of freedom or flexibility characterized the training program in 1963-64 than was previously the case.

Of the fifteen faculty members who felt that methods reforms were the most significant change, six specified changes in the training colleges' methods courses per se. There was general agreement that the rigid adherence to the time-honored Herbartian Steps of preparation, presentation, association, generalization and application, which was partially responsible for the extreme formalism of the classroom, had been replaced by a more flexible approach characterized by an increased emphasis on the learner vis-a-vis the subject matter. This was evidenced by an advocacy of greater student participation in the classroom and the use of methods and materials which were appropriate to the objectives of the particular unit being studied.

Three of the fifteen faculty members, who agreed that significant change had occurred in the methods employed by the training colleges, felt the reform in the methods of student evaluation to be the most significant. This reform was two-fold; in the first instance the training colleges were given a share of the responsibility for evaluating the students' work in the theoretical portion of the curriculum, rather than the entire evaluation being based on the final, university administered, B. Ed. examination. This took place

[29] Appendix VII, Faculty Interview.

in the 1956 curriculum revision when twenty per cent of the grade was assigned to the colleges.[30] A second reform was the institution of a policy whereby the evaluation of the student's teaching ability would be based upon his total practice teaching experience instead of one performance at the end of the year as was previously the case.

It was felt that the termination of the examination lesson resulted in considerably more effort being put into all of the practice lessons in addition to avoiding the stress which naturally attended this final examination lesson. By the same token, the beginnings made in internal or college assessment were felt to result in increased student efforts throughout the term rather than relying entirely upon cramming for the final examination for success in the program.[31]

Two of the faculty members felt that the introduction of guidance and social education and, more specifically, the helping relationship and variety of methods, particularly the use of visual aids, extolled in these courses, was the most significant change to have taken place in the training colleges during the previous decade.

One faculty member considered the introduction of a hobbies period in the training colleges, in order to prepare the prospective teachers for conducting club activities in the secondary schools, to be the most important change. These hobby periods, in which the students spend an hour per week in activities of their own choice such as Indian music or crafts, science, mathematics or dramatics, can be seen as a direct response to the Mudaliar recommendation that there be "training in one or more cocurricular activities for each teacher"[32] and the broader recommendation that community life be encouraged through the promotion of activities within the school and the community.[33] To achieve this latter goal, the report recommends residential training colleges.[34] Although two of the three training colleges, St. Xaviers and S.T.C., maintain hostels, owing to the fact that the colleges are essentially city institutions with most of the students living within commuting distance, it is

[30] *St. Xavier's Handbook,* p. 41.

[31] For an extended discussion of internal assessment and examination reform in general see *Training Colleges and Examination Reform* (New Delhi : National Council of Educational Research and Training, 1963), particularly pp. 9-11.

[32] *Mudaliar Report,* p. 136.

[33] *Ibid.,* p. 139.

[34] *Ibid.*

inconceivable that these colleges should take on a residential character. This fact, coupled with the general belief that the present time allotted to the B. Ed. syllabus is insufficient and the lack of ability of either the colleges or the students to afford the costs which such activities often imply, all mitigate against the development of an extensive extracurricular program.

Another faculty member described the most significant change in the training colleges in the realm of methods as the application of the theories and findings of philosophy and psychology to the training of teachers. In this person's view the "gap between theory and practice" which the Mudaliar Report felt "vitiates training colleges assuming a role of leadership in educational construction,"[35] had at least begun to be bridged.

Finally, two of the fifteen faculty members characterized the change in methods in the training colleges in terms of the relationship between faculty members and trainees. Not only did these faculty members consider this relationship less formal than was the case in the past, they felt that faculty members evidenced a great deal more willingness to help the students with their academic, professional and even personal problems.

Of the nine faculty members who did not consider the most significant change in the training colleges to be in the area of methods, three respondents stated that they felt there had not been any significant change in the methods used or advocated by the training colleges. Such a disavowal of change on the part of the generally more pessimistic faculty members might on the surface appear irreconcilable with the preponderant claims of change and perhaps should lessen the credence of the views expressed by the majority. One is led to suspect that faculty members responded according to their hopes or the plans for these institutions rather than reality. The safest generalization to be made is that afforded by considering the change as a matter of degree. The objective evidence of changes in curriculum and evaluation, and the opinions of the faculty members combined, certainly attest to some progress in the general area of methods' reforms.

While concrete manifestations of reform in the training colleges' methods and curriculum can be identified, the third dimension of reform, the improvement of the quality of instruction, does not present such an optimistic picture. To bring about reform in this

[35] *Ibid.*, p. 141.

area, the Mudaliar Commission advocated the upgrading of both student and faculty qualifications and the development of the advanced study of education.

With regard to the level of students, several events or tendencies apparently are hindering the efforts of the training colleges to secure more highly qualified applicants. These include the low and allegedly declining status of the secondary teacher, the general deterioration of university standards, and the high cost of the B. Ed. program relative to the wealth of the students and the economic benefits of obtaining the degree.

The quality of the persons attracted to the teaching profession is influenced by the status of the profession which, particularly in the case of males, is quite low in India. A survey of college students in the senior Bachelor of Arts (B. A.) and Bachelor of Science (B. Sc.) programs revealed that teaching ranked ninth as a career choice behind businessmen, social workers, professors, journalists, lawyers, doctors, engineers and agriculturalists in that order. For women, teaching ranked second only to social work. This, the author felt, was due to the limited career opportunities available to women.[36]

Traditionally, the teacher has occupied a place of esteem in Indian society. With the advent of Western education this status remained unaltered. In 1875, the Brahmin caste accounted for approximately seventy-five percent of the secondary teachers in the Bombay Presidency, and the salaries were reportedly equal to those of secondary teachers in England. Relative to the cost of living, the Indian secondary teacher was probably the highest paid in the world.[37] As the economic forces of a market society rather than tradition began regulating the distribution of social rewards,[38] the power and prestige of the social classes was rearranged,[39] relegating the teacher to a position considerably below those in commercial and industrial fields.

Among Indian educators, and those in Bombay in particular, it is conceded that the standards of the university are declining. This

[36] S. Panandikar, *The Teacher in India Today* (New Delhi : Ministry of Education, Government of India, 1957), pp. 5-8.

[37] *The Bombay Educational Record*, Vol. XI (Bombay : Education Society's Press, June, 1875), pp. 124-125.

[38] Robert L. Heilbroner, *The Making of Economic Society* (Englewood Cliffs, N. J. : Prentice-Hall, Inc., 1962), p. 43.

[39] *Ibid.*, p. 62.

is seen as the result of the great increase in numbers attending the university. From the point of view of the universities this expansion is unfortunate, but evidently they are unable to withstand the economic and political pressures which attend the popular demand for university admission.[40-41] A lowering of university standards naturally results in a lowering of the standards of the B. Ed. candidate unless relatively stronger graduates can be attracted to the teacher training program.

To make the B. Ed. program more attractive and to ensure that financial need did not preclude the attendance of those otherwise qualified, the Mudaliar Report recommended that,

"no fees should be charged in the training colleges and all student-teachers should be given suitable stipends by the state during the period of training." It further suggested "that teachers already in service should be given during the period of training the same salary which they were getting [as teachers]. They should be expected to execute a bond to serve as teachers for a period of five years."[42]

At present, only about fifteen per cent of the students receive stipends, and about five per cent receive their training tuition free. Even in S. T. C. where financial assistance is somewhat more available due to the fact that it is a state institution, it does not appear very likely that the B. Ed. program will become less of an economic burden for the vast majority of students. Not only does the cost of the B. Ed. program, which ranges from Rs. 250 to Rs. 300, represent a financial sacrifice at the time of study, the salary benefit for acquiring the degree of approximately Rs. 25 per annum is scarcely sufficient to attract candidates on economic grounds.

The suggestion that in-service teachers receive regular salary during their year of absence in return for a commitment to return to their place of employment has generally not been met with in practice. In one high school in which this recommendation is being

[40] Rhona Ghate, "Indian Universities in Transition," *Universities Quarterly*, XIV (February-April, 1960), pp. 150-155.
[41] C. D. Desmukh, "The Crucial Issue in Indian Higher Education," *Asian Survey*, I (July, 1961). Desmukh suggests a dual track system in higher education as a means of simultaneously maintaining standards and expanding.
[42] *Mudaliar Report*, p. 138.

followed, the teachers do not take advantage of the opportunity for the ostensible reason that it binds them to a five-year contract.[43] In this connection it should be mentioned that one of the reasons for pursuing the B.Ed. degree, aside from the incentive of acquiring the degree for its own sake, is the expectation of "promotion" from a middle school to a high school teaching position or an eventual promotion to an administrative position.

Mindful of the brevity of the B. Ed. program, the Mudaliar Commission suggested that the candidates be selected several months in advance in order that they could begin background reading preparation which would be recommended by the individual universities.[44] This suggestion has not been followed. Aside from the problems of the cost and the availability of books, there is considerable reason to doubt that students would comply with such a requirement. Many of the comments of the faculty members corroborated the impression that the B. Ed. students did very little purposeful reading, particularly in English.

The level of English proficiency of the B. Ed. candidates is undoubtedly a major factor in the quality of the program. From 1960 to 1970 a preponderance of the B. Ed. candidates will have studied English as a foreign language for only four years in the secondary schools in addition to their university training in English. This is the result of the post-independence decision, put into effect in 1948, not to offer English until Standard VIII. This policy remained in effect until 1960 when, once again, English was offered from Standard V.[45]

Although the Mudaliar Commission recommended that English be offered from Standard V,[46] at the same time it placed a great deal of stress on learning Hindi as a national language, and the regional language in those cases in which it was other than Hindi, as well. Furthermore, the report left the door open for the eventual replacement of English by an Indian language through the suggestion that sufficient work of a high quality in a native medium be produced in order that it could be used as the language of higher instruction in lieu of English.[47] It would have been impolitic

[43] Interview with J. Desai, Principal, G. T. High School, March 13, 1964.
[44] *Mudaliar Report*, p. 139.
[45] Interview with Professor M. Y. Bhide, February 18, 1964.
[46] *Mudaliar Report*, p. 60.
[47] *Ibid.*

for the Commission to have recommended otherwise, for, in the interest of promoting nationalism, the displacement of English at the higher levels of education has consistently been advocated by many Indians.[48]

In the selection of students for the B. Ed. program the two most important criteria used are the class[49] of university degree and the length of teaching experience.[50] All students are required to be graduates of either Bombay University or a university approved by Bombay University. Ideally, the training colleges would like to attract at least second class graduates, for it is tacitly understood that the secondary teaching field cannot hope to attract first class graduates. Perhaps, as a result of rationalization, there is some doubt as to whether first class graduates make the best teachers and, in the same vein of thought, whether, in fact, second class graduates make better teachers than do third class graduates.

TABLE 4

EDUCATIONAL QUALIFICATIONS OF THE BACHELOR OF EDUCA-TION STUDENTS IN THE SECONDARY TRAINING COLLEGE[51]

	M.A.	B.A. I	B.A. II	B.A. III	B.Sc. I	B.Sc. II	B.Sc. III	TOTAL
1910-11	2	0	0	24	0	0	0	31[a]
1920-21	4	0	4	22	0	0	0	30
1930-31	2	0	13	33	0	5	7	60
1940-41	20	0	14	44	0	11	10	99
1950-51	13	1	24	37	0	7	16	99[b]
1963-64	7	3	31	22	0	6	16	85

[a] Class of 1910-11 included five non-university graduates.

[b] Class of 1950-51 included one Bachelor of Commerce Graduate.

[48] "Forging National Unity," *Times Educational Supplement*, No. 2424 (November 3, 1961), p. 598.

[49] Graduates of the university fall into either first class, second or pass (III) class categories. These categories roughly correspond to a minimum average of ninety, eighty and seventy percent respectively used in many American colleges. Incidentally, the evaluation of examinations in India is based on zero rather than 100 percent.

[50] The information contained in the remaining discussion of the student in this section was obtained in the student questionnaire. (See Appendix VIII).

[51] Sidhwa, "Training of Secondary Teachers in the State of Bombay," pp. 37-43 for years 1910-11 through 1950-51. Figures for 1963-64 compiled from student questionnaire.

Table 4 on page 51 indicates the educational qualifications of S. T. C.'s B. Ed. candidates for selected years from 1910-11 to 1963-64. The proportion of second class B. A. graduates has continuously increased to the point where they now outnumber the third class B. A. graduates who enter the B. Ed. program. Nonetheless, third class B. A. graduates continue to come into the program in significant numbers.

The trend toward higher qualifications of B. A. graduates does not hold for B. Sc. graduates, who, owing to the market demand for their skills, are considerably more difficult to attract to teaching than the B. A. graduates. Furthermore, the total number of B. Sc. graduates in the B. Ed. program had declined since the 1940-41 period. Considering the increasing demand for science teachers at the secondary level, this dearth of B. Ed. candidates with a degree in science represents one of the most crucial problems currently facing the training colleges.[52]

The number of applicants rejected exceeds the number admissible threefold, and those not accepted are normally advised to acquire further teaching experience. A divergence of views with regard to the amount of teaching experience desirable exists among the institutions, for, while one principal considers three years to be an optimum length, another apparently assumes that the length of teaching experience is in direct proporation to the candidate's qualification; that is, the greater the number of years of experience, the better qualified the candidate is felt to be.

It is commonly believed the applicants lacking any teaching experience cannot derive full benefit from the B. Ed. program since they are unable to relate its theoretical content to any personal experience. Candidates with experience are also preferred for the very practical reason that those without experience are required to present fifty-five practice lessons instead of the regularly required thirty, thus increasing the staff's supervisory duties.

Table 5 indicates the number of years of teaching experience of the 1963-64 B. Ed. candidates. This table clearly reveals the successful results of the training colleges' insistence upon prior teaching experience and the considerable extent of teaching experience which many candidates obtain before entering the program.

[52] Interview with Fr. A. Solagran, May 8, 1964.

TABLE 5

TEACHING EXPERIENCE OF BOMBAY UNIVERSITY
BACHELOR OF EDUCATION CANDIDATES, 1963-64

Years Experience	S. T. C.	St. Xavier's	Sadhana	Total	Per cent of Total
0	2	0	4	6	2·7%
1	29	57	21	107	48·4%
2-5	37	31	9	77	34·8%
6 and over	12	6	13	31	14 %

A further problem with regard to the preparation of the B. Ed. students is the difficulty in obtaining secondary teachers with college training in their particular teaching subject. This problem stems from the basic fact that many of the subjects offered in the secondary schools are not offered at the college level and vice versa.[53] Furthermore, many students whose previous education was not geared to entering the teaching profession, enter the B. Ed. program. Of the two hundred and seventy students who participated in the student questionnaire, seventy-four, or 27·4%, made their decision to become teachers after they had received their college degree. These students are naturally less likely to have appropriate college backgrounds for secondary teaching. It is particularly common among the male students to find the decision to enter the teaching profession made after working in other occupations. Forty-three of the ninety-seven male students, or 44%, indicated that they had held full time jobs other than teaching prior to entering the B. Ed. program, while twelve of the one hundred and twenty-two females, or 10%, were previously so employed.

Considerable emphasis is given to the maturity of prospective candidates, which is probably the most highly valued subjective student characteristic. One of the training colleges interviews all of its prospective candidates to arrive at some judgment of the candidate's maturity and potential to benefit from the B.Ed. program.

[53] See Appendixes IV and II for the university and high school curricula respectively.

The generally held view is that the candidate fresh from the university is immature, and the desired maturity is gained as a by-product of the teaching experience which is virtually required by the training colleges.

Previous employment, both in teaching and other occupations, helps account for the relatively advanced age of the B.Ed. student as depicted in Table 6.

TABLE 6

AGE OF BOMBAY UNIVERSITY BACHELOR OF EDUCATION CANDIDATES BY SEX, 1963-64 [54]

Age	Female	Male	Total
20	3	0	3
21-25	83	13	96
26-30	28	54	82
31-35	15	28	43
36 and over	4[a]	3	7
Total	133	98	231

[a] Three of the females in the 36 and over category are married women who decided to embark upon teaching careers to supplement the family income. The entrance of housewives into teaching is a recent innovation and may presage a future trend.

One normally completes his secondary schooling at the age of sixteen or seventeen and his college education at age nineteen or twenty. The obvious tendency for the male to enter the program at a later age than the female is primarily the result of the male's greater dependence on the income from teaching, or other forms of employment, which is interrupted for one year by the B. Ed. program.

The extent to which B.Ed. students find it necessary to be gainfully employed during the academic year, thus detracting from the energies given to the B. Ed. program, is difficult to determine. University regulations forbid students to work while enrolled in the program, yet as many as fifty of the students, or 30%, admitted to giving tuitions, or tutoring students, as indicated in Table 7.

[54] Data compiled from student questionnaire, Appendix VIII.

TABLE 7

STUDENT SOURCES OF INCOME DURING THE BOMBAY
UNIVERSITY BACHELOR OF EDUCATION PROGRAM, 1963-64

Sources of Income	Number of Students	Per cent of Total Responding
None	50	30·5%
Tuitions	50	30·5%
Part-time Teaching	8	4·9%
Loan	2	1·2%
Stipend	24	14·6%
No Response	30	18·3%
Total	164	100 %

Judging from the information given in Table 7, it can be assumed that the training program is a full-time preoccupation for
most of the students, and that the majority of the students are
dependent upon either their personal savings or financial assistance
from members of their families for the tuition and expenses
incurred throughout the program. In order to implement the
Mudaliar Report's recommendations regarding financial assistance for B. Ed. students, it appears that funds from the central
government would be required, for the training colleges are
dependent upon the student's fees for their operation, and there is
apparently little likelihood of additional aid from the state.

With regard to faculty members, the Mudaliar Commission was
considerably more explicit in its recommendation for upgrading
qualifications than was the case with students. The report stipulated that faculty members should have the M. Ed. degree, and a
minimum of three years teaching experience in the secondary
schools. It further stated that faculty members should have either
a first class or honors degree[55] at the B. A. or B. Sc. level or a
Master's degree in the academic field in which they were teaching
methods courses.[56]

These latter recommendations regarding academic subject matter
qualifications are generally not being met in the training colleges

[55] An honors degree signifies a higher quality of college work than the regular
degree program. Entrance requirements for the honors program are higher
than for regular university entrance, the degree examination covers a greater
quantity of subjects and to claim an honors degree the candidate must receive
at least a second class in the degree examinations.

[56] *Mudaliar Report,* p. 140.

of Bombay University. None of the twenty-four faculty members reported receiving first class subject matter degree. Only seven of the twenty-four had honors degrees and these were evenly distributed among the faculty members with regard to length of teaching experience, thus suggesting the absence of any significant change in faculty qualifications since the issuance of the Mudaliar report.

By contrast to the Mudaliar recommendations, the faculty members of Bombay University are presently required to have a second class college degree.[57] Further work beyond the Bachelor's degree is not required, nor does the university require that the faculty member's academic degree be in the subject in which he teaches methods courses. In addition to being at least a second class graduate, Bombay University's training college faculty members must possess the following requirements :

1. At least a second class teaching degree.
2. At least a second class Master of Education.
3. At least three years teaching or administrative experience in the high schools.[58]

TABLE 8

DEGREES IN EDUCATION OF THE BOMBAY UNIVERSITY TRAINING COLLEGE FACULTY MEMBERS

	B.Ed.	M.Ed.	Ph. D. in Education
Number	23[a]	19	6[b]
Percent of Total	95·8%	78·3%	25%

[a] The single faculty member without a B. Ed. was one of two faculty members who had had previous experience in an arts college. Presumably, this experience offset his lack of training in education. His duties at the training college consisted of the coaching and supervision of practice teachers in addition to his language teaching.

[b] Two of the faculty members are currently writing Ph. D. theses in education under the supervision of senior faculty members.

[57] Interview with N.R. Parasnis, Principal, Secondary Training College, May 25, 1964. An exception to the requirement for a second class college degree is made and a third class degree is permitted if the candidate has a M.A. in his teaching subject; e.g., a Master's degree in Hindi for one who instructs in the methods of Hindi.

[58] Ibid.

In practice, the university's requirements are largely being met in the three training colleges. Table 8 indicates the degrees in education acquired by the twenty-four faculty members (of a total of twenty-six) interviewed from three training colleges.

With regard to academic or subject matter background, all of the faculty members held either a B.A. or B. Sc. degree. Of those faculty members engaged in teaching special methods courses, all but three had at least a Bachelor's degree in their particular special methods subject. Table 9 indicates the degrees in academic fields attained by the twenty-two faculty members engaged in teaching special methods courses.

TABLE 9

ACADEMIC DEGREES OF THE BOMBAY UNIVERSITY
TRAINING COLLEGE FACULTY MEMBERS TEACHING COURSES
IN SPECIAL METHODS

	B.A. or B.Sc.	M.A.	Ph. D.
Number with Degree in Special Methods Subject	19	10	1
Percent of Total Teaching Special Methods Courses	84·4%	45·5%	4·5%

A further analysis of the academic background of the training college faculty reveals a marked bias in favor of language training and corresponding deficiency in training in science and mathematics. Only three of the faculty members had a B.Sc. degree. Of the remaining twenty-one faculty members, all of whom had a B. A. degree, only one had offered mathematics as a major. Of the ten faculty members with Masters degrees, eight were in language, one in history and one in geography.[59] Thus, there is a total absence of faculty members with advanced training in the sciences or mathematics in the training colleges.

With regard to experimental background, 95. 8 percent (twenty-three of twenty-four) of the training college faculty members have

[59] Five of the training college faculty members have studied in foreign institutions. Three of these hold certificates or diplomas from English universities, one from a Canadian university and one holds a Master's degree in geography from Northwestern University in the United States.

had teaching experience at the secondary level. The length of such experience ranges from one to fifteen years, and the average number of years of experience is seven. In addition to secondary teaching experience, 33·3 percent of the faculty members have held secondary school administrative posts, 20 percent have held inspector or research positions with the Maharashtra Department of Public Instruction, and 12·5 percent (three of twenty-four) have had post-secondary teaching experience.

None of the present faculty members have had any experience at other secondary training colleges, and the median length of service in the training colleges is slightly over eight years.[60] Only two of the faculty members interviewed expressed a desire to do other than remain in their present capacities until retirement. One of these, a senior professor, expressed an ambition to become a training college principal, and the second, a relatively young faculty member, spoke of a possible interest in going into industry where it was felt there would be a demand for his particular educational background in the field of counseling.

While there appeared to be very little interest in movement with regard to one's particular position, there was considerable interest in opportunities to go abroad for further study and to learn about foreign educational practices. The United States appeared to be the first choice for this purpose and Great Britain, the second. One faculty member was interested in pursuing his studies in Austria and one expressed a desire to study in any Asian country. Undoubtedly, the interviewer's United States origin influenced both the expression of interest in foreign research and the preferred locations for this research in a positive direction.

Probably the principal barrier to attracting highly qualified individuals to the training college faculties is an economic one. The salaries of the training college faculties are low by any standards. Male faculty members with families to support, and nearly all except the three religious faculty members of St. Xavier's are supporting a family, find their salaries extremely meager, particularly when the relatively high and ever-increasing costs of living in the urban area of Bombay are considered. By contrast, the female faculty members view their salaries as a supplement to the family

[60] The Sadhana School of Educational Research and Training is excepted from this particular consideration owing to the fact that it has only been in existence for three years.

income with the result that they are much less apt to be discontent with their income.

Aside from the problem of meeting living costs, the relative income of university and training college teachers is a particular ground for complaint. As demonstrated in Table 10 the salary received by university professors is considerably higher than that of the training college faculty. The latter feel that when all things are considered, particularly the hours that they work, they should be compensated on at least an equal basis with their university counterparts, and some of them have expressed the view that they should receive even higher salaries.

TABLE 10

COMPARISON OF TRAINING COLLEGE AND BOMBAY UNIVERSITY FACULTY SALARIES, 1963-64[61]

	Training College				University		
	Low	High	Median		Low	High	Median
Assistant				Lecturer	400	800	600
Lecturer	250	300	275				
Lecturer	290	525	401	Reader	700	1100	900
Professor	429	590	510	Professor	1000	1500	1250

Criticism of the training college faculty salaries is tempered somewhat by the persisting view that teaching is an altruistic profession calling for a spirit of sacrifice and a lack of concern for worldly gain. One of the principals expressed the view that discontentment with the salary scale is in exceedingly poor taste and would only be voiced by one unfit to be a member of the profession. Evidence exists, however, that this attitude is diminishing. For example, when one faculty member left his position to accept a headmaster's position in a secondary school for a salary approximately twice as large as that he was receiving, the expressed reaction of his training college colleagues was one of approbation.

One of the essential ingredients for a more highly qualified training college faculty is the continued development of a program in the advanced study of pedagogy. As previously noted, the study

[61] Salary figures given represent rupees per month. The source of figures for the university pay scale was an interview with A. Soares, Assistant Registrar, Bombay University. A formal statement of the training college faculty salaries was not available. These salaries were compiled on the basis of data obtained in the faculty interview.

of education beyond the B.Ed. level is a relatively recent development in Bombay University; the M. Ed. degree having been instituted in 1936 and the Ph. D. in Education in 1941.[62] At present, study in education beyond the B. Ed. level is conducted exclusively in training colleges. The Indian Institute of Education was established for the purpose of conducting research and preparing students for advanced education degrees in 1948, but this short-lived institution was gradually abandoned and ceased to function completely after 1960.[63]

The M. Ed. degree program is open to all students who have a B. Ed. degree. It may be taken by thesis alone or by study of a program of M. Ed. courses, combined with a dissertation.[64] The M. Ed. course of studies, which came into effect in 1957, consists of three compulsory papers ; Philosophy of Education, Advanced Educational psychology and Methodology of Research, and two papers selected from Administration of Education, Educational Thought, and Experimental Education. None of the aforementioned areas of study include more than one basic course, and, as the breadth of such a program suggests, there is very little specialization in the M. Ed. program.

The Master's level courses are taught by the senior faculty members from all three of the training colleges who, in most instances, serve as guides approved by the university for supervising the thesis work of M. Ed. and Ph. D. candidates. The quality of scholarship exhibited in the theses is generally considered to be low. The doctoral theses evidenced such apparent shortcomings as lack of continuity, inconsistency in reasoning, and failure to evaluate sources critically, but were, nonetheless, of considerably higher quality than the Master's theses.[65]

When one considers that, for the most part, training college faculty members have not received any training in education beyond the Master's degree, it becomes apparent that there is a need for

[62] Naik, *A Review of Education in Bombay State*, p. 288.

[63] Interview with A. S. Sthalekar. The reasons for the demise of the Institute would be of interest; however, interviews with various Bombay educational officials, including some of the previous members of the Institute's staff only revealed that the staff members moved elsewhere. Inadequate financial support undoubtedly was a contributing factor.

[64] *St. Xavier's Handbook*, p. 65.

[65] This judgment is based on a reading of several M. Ed. and Ph. D. theses in education written in Bombay University.

higher quality and more advanced work in the field of education as well as an upgrading of the faculty members' academic qualifications. The newly created M. Ed. syllabus, a response to the Mudaliar Commission's recommendation that

> "post-graduate courses in education are needed to learn modern methods followed in different countries, to cultivate aptitude for research so that experiments on new methods and techniques of education suited to the country and the community may be undertaken, . . . and to train headmasters, inspectors and the teaching staff of training institutions",[66]

is a hopeful beginning, but this consideration of the background of the faculty members poses the uncomfortable problem of whether or not the training colleges are suitably staffed to perform this task.

By contrast to the nebulous and largely negative picture that emerges from a consideration of the attempts to raise the quality of instruction in the training colleges, in the fourth and final category of reform to be considered, the development of in-service education, definite forward strides have been made. Under the sponsorship of the All India Council for Secondary Education (A. I. C. S. E.) an Extension Services Program was begun in 1955. Since the inspection of this program, ninety-two Extension Services Centers have been established throughout India.[67] The program, which is financed by the Ford Foundation and the Technical Cooperation Mission, is designed to provide in-service training for teachers in order to equip them with the knowledge and skills needed to operate in a multipurpose school.

In 1960 an Extension Services Center was established in Bombay.[68]

---

[66] *Mudaliar Report*, p. 139.

[67] Interview with A. C. Devegowda, Director, Directorate of Extension Programs for Secondary Education, New Delhi, January 25, 1964. For a general discussion of Extension Programs consult : S. Doraiswami, *Extension Services Project in India* (New Delhi : Directorate of Extension Programs for Secondary Education, Government of India, 1961) and Ivan G. Fay, *Notes on Extension in Agriculture* (Bombay : Asia Publishing House, 1962).

[68] *Education in Maharashtra, Annual Administration Report, 1959-60*, p. 36. In this connection it should also be noted that St. Xavier's has a program of service to secondary schools, although it is not included in the national count of extension centers, and it does not accept the Central Government's funds for its operation.

This center, which services 320 urban secondary schools and 60 schools in rural areas, is administered by the S. T. C., with the principal of the training college serving as the director.[69] However, the responsibility for the actual management of the program resides with a full-time coordinator who works directly with the Directorate of Extension Program for Secondary Education (D. E. P. S. E.).

The activities of the center typically include seminars or workshops on topics relating to the teaching of science, social studies or English. These are held in one of the secondary schools which agrees to act as a host by making the necessary provisions for boarding and lodging the participants throughout the course of the meeting, which might last from one to four days. In addition to the funds allocated by the D. E. P. S. E., the State of Maharashtra lends financial assistance by paying the costs of travel and the living expenses of the participants. The state further assists the extension centers by encouraging the secondary schools to participate in these programs.

The coordinator is responsible for making all the necessary arrangements for these meetings, and the director's participation is limited to ceremonial functions such as the presentation of an opening address. The training college faculty members participate in these programs in some instances, but this participation is not on a continuous basis and involves only a small proportion of the faculty members.[70]

On balance, the extension program represents a highly successful attempt by the educational organs of the central government in cooperation with international agencies to influence Indian education at the grass-roots level. For their part, the training colleges serve as a natural link between the central government's D. E. P. S. E. and the secondary schools.

One minor criticism which might be levelled at the program is the insufficient involvement of the training college as an institution, or the faculty members, and students for that matter, in the activities of the extension center. Nonetheless, the essential purpose of the program—bringing new information regarding subject matter

[69] Doraiswami, *Extension Services Project in India*, Appendix II.

[70] N. R. Parasnis, principal and director, and M. B. Khedkar, coordinator, *Annual Report on the Activities of the Extension Services Department, Bombay, for the year, 1963-64.* (Mimeographed).

and methods of instruction to the in-service teacher—is being accomplished.[71]

It is difficult to assess the impact of such a venture as the extension program by any means short of a systematic detailed inquiry, but the number of individuals and institutions reached by this program and the enthusiasm with which the center's activities are received serve to attest to the value of the extension program.[72] No matter how successful the extension program is in introducing modern curricula and techniques to the secondary schools, it can do no more than contribute to a climate of receptivity for the multipurpose high school. In this way, the extension program is contributing to the eventual fulfilment of the Mudaliar Commission's goals for secondary education more directly than any of the reforms that have been instituted in the training colleges.

Three very important considerations, which help to account for the extension program's success in contradiction to that of the training colleges, should be noted. First, the extension program, being a fresh operation, does not have to overcome the obstacles to change invariably presented by established institutions such as the training colleges. Second, the extension program enjoys not only the direction, but the financial support of a central authority. Finally, the extension program, through the use of various educational methods such as scientific experiments and the use of audio-visual aids, provides a tangible model for effective instruction, which the in-service secondary teachers are, in turn, encouraged to emulate.

This is not to discount the progress made in the training colleges. In retrospect, the reforms advocated by the Mudaliar Commission, particularly the widespread establishment of the multipurpose high school, did not provide the training colleges with very realistic goals. Nonetheless, the Mudaliar Report has exerted an obvious, direct influence on these institutions as evidenced by such developments as the broadening of the curriculum and the de-emphasizing of the B. Ed. examination. Its influence can also be perceived in less concrete developments such as the decline of authoritarianism on the part of the training college staff and the heightened awareness of social problems on the part of both faculty and students.

[71] *Ibid.*
[72] Field Trip, Secondary Training College Extension Program Workshop, Sinnar High School, Sinnar, India, February 22-23, 1964.

CHAPTER IV

THE PRESENT PRACTICES OF BOMBAY UNIVERSITY'S TRAINING COLLEGES, 1963-64

Since the Mudaliar Report provides a clear and comprehensive view of the goals for India's secondary education, it has provided a yardstick by which the progress of the secondary training colleges could be measured. Through the preceding chapters' consideration of the origins and developments of the training colleges with particular emphasis on the ten year period since the issuance of the Mudaliar Report, the accomplishments and the shortcomings of these institutions have been ascertained. Essentially, Bombay University's training colleges have not succeeded in contributing to the major, specific objective stipulated by the report : that of the establishment of the multipurpose high school.

However, when the Report's broader objectives of establishing an educational system which transcends a narrow academic approach and relates the curriculum to the society are considered, it becomes evident that throughout much of their history, and particularly since independence, the training colleges have moved in the direction intended by the Mudaliar Commission.

In the present chapter an effort will be made to determine the extent to which secondary teacher training in Bombay University has become attuned to the ideals envisioned in the Mudaliar Report. This will be accomplished by means of an analysis of the present practices in the training colleges, which were observed throughout the academic year, 1963-64.

It is primarily the intention to present a general picture of secondary teacher training as it pertains to Bombay University ; therefore, an effort will be made to arrive at generalizations which will be applicable to all three of the training colleges. This is entirely feasible as there is a considerable degree of uniformity in the operation of the B. Ed. program from institution to institution, as a result of the overall jurisdiction of Bombay University.

Nonetheless, one fundamental distinction among the training institutions does exist and pervades, albeit to a limited extent, the operation of the individual institutions. This distinction stems from the differences in the form of management among the training colleges. Bombay University's original training institution, Secondary Training College (S. T. C.), is under the auspices of the State of Maharashtra. St. Xavier's Institute of Education and the Sadhana School of Educational Research and Training are privately managed. St. Xavier's, a Jesuit institution, is managed by the Bombay Xavierian Corporation and Sadhana is governed by the Sadhana Education Society.[1] The governing bodies of the private institutions are charged with the responsibility of administering their institutions in accordance with the requirements of Bombay University.[2] In actual practice, however, the governing bodies entrust the operation of their institutions to the principals and their staffs.

The chief concern of the managing bodies is the financing of their respective institutions, for both of the private training colleges rely to a considerable extent on funds contributed by the management. In the case of St. Xavier's, the primary source of funds other than students' fees and state aid is the profits which the Xavierian Corporation realizes from the operation of St. Xavier's College, a liberal arts institution, which it also manages. Sadhana's deficit is met by voluntary donations from the members of the society, ranging from patrons, who contribute at least Rs. 51,000, to ordinary members, who contribute at least Rs. 100 annually or a total of Rs. 1,000.[3] By contrast, all of the operating expenses of S.T.C. not met by income from students' fees are furnished by the state as shown in Table 11.

The disparity in the total cost of operation among the three institutions is primarily due to the difference in physical facilities and, in particular, the building in which they are housed. St.

[1] *The Societies Registration Act* (1860). The term society is used to designate associations organized under the *Societies Registration Act* (1860). This is an act for the registration of literary, scientific and charitable organizations affording them legal status and potentially qualifying their educational institutions for governmental financial support.

[2] *Constitution of St. Xavier's Institute of Education* (In effect as of 1963-64).

[3] *Sadhana Education Society* (Bombay : Jawahir P. Press, n. d.), pp. 7-8.

TABLE 11

BUDGET OF BOMBAY UNIVERSITY'S
TRAINING COLLEGES, 1962-63[4]

Institution	Income from Students' Fees	Income from State	Income from Private Sources	Yearly Cost of Operation
	Rs.	Rs.	Rs.	Rs.
Secondary Training College	28,000·00	80,958·00		108,985·00
St. Xavier's	85,070·00	39,199·00	41,106·91	165,375·91
Sadhana	25,640·00	16,941·55	20,735·00	63,316·55

Xavier's rents a modern four-story building equipped with an elevator, while Sadhana occupies temporary quarters consisting of two makeshift classrooms, which were originally intended to serve as a cafeteria and lounge for the employees of a tuberculosis hospital adjoining the college. S.T.C. might be said to occupy a position between these extremes with regard to its building and facilities. It is housed in an imposing rococo structure suggestive of a faded elegance; an impression that is reinforced by the nonfunctional aspect of its interior, the lack of modern accoutrements and its generally worn condition.

While each of the three training colleges is overseen by a board of directors, or in the case of S.T.C., by the State Director of Education, the principals, nonetheless, have relative autonomy in the supervision of the day to day operation of their institutions. The manner in which the principals administer their institutions varies, but this appears to be largely the result of the predilection of the individual principal rather than policy controls attributable to the directors.

[4] Figures were obtained from certified copies of the annual income and expenditure accounts of the three institutions for the year ending March 31, 1963. Fees for Bachelor of Education students including tuition, various services charges and university examination fees, range from Rs. 250 to Rs. 300. Students' fees for St. Xavier's indicated above include the fees from the Diploma of Education program and were not available for the Bachelor's program exclusively.

In addition to the many supervisory and ceremonial tasks, all of the principals are engaged in teaching and directing the research of Master's and Ph. D. candidates. The extent to which the principals delegate their duties varies considerably, but they all enlist the aid of the faculty members to some extent. An enumeration of the duties delegated by the S.T.C. principal will serve to illustrate the various administrative tasks confronted by the principal :

Vice-principal —in charge of Master of Education and lecture series.

One professor —in charge of social and cultural activities.

Two professors—in charge of the timetable for the practice teaching.

One professor —in charge of lecture, essay and examination timetable.

One professor —in charge of educational visits and picnics.[5]

In general, while the principal calls on his staff for various kinds of assistance, thus suggesting a maximum amount of cooperation, he nonetheless exercises virtually complete control over his staff, and his directives go unquestioned. Faculty views are expressed when requested, but these are invariably in accord with the principal's wishes. In a word, the relationship between the principal and his staff is marked by a high degree of respect.[6]

The principals have the major voice in the hiring of new faculty members for their institutions, particularly in the private training colleges.[7] The faculty members of S.T.C. are employees of the state and, as such, are subject to assignment in whatever capacity the state may direct. As a result, the S.T.C. faculty tends to be recruited from administrative positions such as inspector's posts or possibly from teaching positions in the state's primary teacher

---

[5] Interview with N. R. Parasnis, June 16, 1964.

[6] This observation is primarily based on attendance at faculty meetings at two of the training colleges.

[7] Interview with N. R. Parasnis, June 16, 1964. In the instance of S. T. C. this voice is quite indirect ; the principal directs requests for faculty members to the State Director of Education, who, in turn, forwards the request to the State Public Services Commission which publicly advertises the post. As a member of this Commission which is charged with the selection of the best candidate, the principal has a considerable voice in the ultimate selection of the candidate for the faculty position.

training institutions; whereas the faculty of St. Xavier's and Sadhana are much more likely to be selected from among the particularly promising graduate students of these institutions.

The authority exercised by the principal, although reportedly less rigid than in the past, would appear to be a constraining influence on the innovative and experimental efforts which the Mudaliar Commission advocates for secondary education. Paradoxically, the report does not suggest any deviation from the authoritarian pattern of administration presently found in the training colleges. Although it does not address itself specifically to the exercise of authority by the principal or the relationship between the principal and the training college staff, it does advocate increased discipline on the part of the secondary school staffs as a means of promoting student discipline and speaks of "the limitations within which teachers must act for the best interests of the profession".[8]

The absence of opportunities for faculty members to exercise leadership in the training college enterprise, coupled with the demands placed upon their time, by training college duties and the outside activities needed to supplement their income, all serve to deter them from activities or research which would foster changes and improvements in the training colleges or contribute to their individual competencies.

Owing to the detailed attention given to the practical phase of the curriculum, the largest portion of the faculty member's time and effort is devoted to counseling, coaching and criticising the efforts of the trainees in order to help them develop proper teaching techniques. Throughout both terms of the B. Ed. program, each of the faculty members spends two hours and a quarter daily working with a group of twelve students.

The usual faculty teaching load consists of a special methods course and a course in one of the theoretical branches of education. For example, a faculty member might offer a course in the methods of teaching English and the history of Indian education. This represents approximately four hours per week during which faculty members are engaged in actual classroom instruction. In addition to instruction, supervision of practical work and the previously noted administrative duties, ten of the twelve male faculty members[9] and

---

[8] *Mudaliar Report,* p. 102.

[9] The religious faculty members of St. Xavier's were not included in this particular consideration.

two of the seven female faculty members reported that they held examiner's positions. This entails the evaluation of B. Ed., Dip. Ed., or in some cases, the Secondary School Certificate (S.S.C.) examinations of students other than those enrolled in the examiner's particular institution.[10]

Although the heavy institutional demands on the faculty members and the time which they devote to examinerships permits very little opportunity for research or related academic activity, these reasons, alone, do not fully account for the lack of such activity. Neither the university administration nor the training college principals appear to encourage or reward research, nor is there any apparent expectancy that such activity should be considered a part of the faculty member's responsibility.

Rigid adherence to the B. Ed. syllabus, a contributing cause of the lack of research and experimentation on the part of faculty members, operates to the detriment of the student's learning experience as well. Throughout the entire ten months of the B. Ed. program the candidate pursues the time-honored program of practical work and theoretical study prescribed by Bombay University.

The practical portion of the curriculum is divided into four phases, which are designed to familiarize the candidate with correct teaching procedures and gradually provide him with the practical experience required to bring him to the desired level of teaching proficiency. In the initial phase correct teaching methods are explained to the candidate in great detail. Special emphasis is given to the rules for planning lessons and using visual aids, particularly the blackboard.[11]

The second phase of the practical curriculum consists of the observation of regular secondary school classes. The trainees keep a "diary" containing notes on their observation which is evaluated

[10] The usual remuneration for examiners is approximately Rs. 500 per annum, although one faculty member, a chief examiner for both the B. Ed. and S. S. C. examinations, reported an annual income of Rs. 1500 from this source. This dependence of the faculty members on examinerships for abetting their salaries is analogous to the secondary school teacher's usual means of supplementing his income by tutoring students.

[11] D. Rao, G. H. Dhupkar et al. Teaching Commerce in the Multipurpose Secondary School (New Delhi : Directorate of Extension Programmes for Secondary Education, 1962), p. 9. The thirteen rules for the use of the blackboard cited in this booklet serve to illustrate the elaborate detail which characterizes the work leading up to the practice teaching experience.

by a faculty member. Discussions are held throughout this phase to ensure that the lessons are being carefully observed and the trainee is acquiring a grasp of correct teaching methods.

In the third and crucial portion of the practical curriculum, the trainee begins his actual practice teaching. Prior to this the students present demonstration lessons before fellow trainees. These lessons are thoroughly critiqued by the students and the faculty supervisor before preparation begins for the first practice lesson. After several rehearsals, the student, accompanied by a faculty member, is prepared to present what invariably and understandably is a polished performance for a first lesson, his years of prior teaching experience notwithstanding.

The fourth and final phase of the practical work consists of a written critique by the faculty member who observes the practice lesson and a tutorial, or group discussion, of the strengths and weaknesses of the lesson. This is followed by a period of further practice for each of the ensuing lessons. This process is continued throughout the term until the candidate has presented thirty lessons.

An account of the practice lessons should furnish an illustration of the methods extolled in the training colleges, for these lessons represent the culmination of the practical training and, presumably, include the application of the methods advocated in the teacher's training. The method used in these lessons has been aptly termed the "question and answer method,"[12] for the major difference between the lecture method employed in the training college and a class taught by a practice teacher is the frequent use of questions throughout the latter's presentation.

The use of this method was evidenced in both the Standard V arithmetic class and the Standard VII social studies class reported on here. In the arithmetic class the lesson was entitled "Factors and Multiples." Instruction was given solely by example. The teacher wrote on the blackboard "$5 \times 2 = 10$" and then explained to the class that "5" and "2" were the factors and "10" the multiple. He then wrote other similar examples on the board and asked various student volunteers to identify the factors and the multiples. When pupils responded incorrectly, there was no attempt made to determine the reason for their error ; rather, the question

---

[12] A. H. Mulla, "Difficulties of Secondary Teachers in the State of Bombay" (unpublished Master of Education thesis, Bombay University, 1954), p. 218.

would be repeated until the correct answer was elicited. During the lesson, one question was asked which none of the students were able to answer, whereupon the practice teacher turned to the supervising faculty member, seated in the rear of the classroom, for guidance. The supervisor rephrased the question and promptly received the correct answer.

Very similarly, in the social studies class, where the topic was the life of Zoroaster, the teacher recited a few principal facts about the subject's life and then asked questions to ensure that these could be recalled by the students. Specific responses were required, and when students began to answer in a way which differed from the material as it was presented by the instructor, the students were told to sit down and another volunteer was asked to reply. The facts of Zoroaster's life were related without regard for their social or religious importance, and any significance of Zoroaster's life for the students was not mentioned.

In sum, these classes appeared to provide very little evidence to refute the various charges levelled at secondary teaching to the effect that it is mechanical or stereotyped and fails to bring out independent and critical thinking. The practice teacher displayed a degree of confidence bordering on arrogance, which apparently stemmed from his thorough familiarity with the material being presented and the manner in which it was to be presented. Careful attention was given to the well-rehearsed plan for the lesson and very little empathy was displayed toward the students. The performance of the practice teachers did not appear to differ from the approach of the traditional secondary school teacher to which they had been accustomed as pupils.[13]

By the same token, the training colleges continue to adhere to the lecture as the virtually exclusive method of transmitting knowledge in the theoretical portion of the curriculum. The only departure from lecturing comes in the form of an occasional question to the class for the purpose of emphasizing a particular point. The atmosphere in the classroom is always quite formal. Normally, the students are all assembled and in their seats when the lecturer arrives. The lecturer calls the roll with each student responding, "Present, sir." When the bell sounds denoting the end of the

---

[13] These observations are based on frequent and sustained contact with all aspects of the training program and attendance at several of the practice lessons, in particular.

period, the lecturer and students proceed directly from the class-room to the next class without any discussion of the lecture either with the lecturer or among the students.

Throughout the lecture, students are generally attentive and occupied with taking notes. The material presented strictly adheres to the prescribed syllabus, which, in turn, is the basis for the B. Ed. examination. Frequently, the lecturer will make it explicit that a certain point of information is likely to appear on the examination.

When not dealing with material in the syllabus, the lecturer indulges in what might euphemistically be called wisdom teaching. This is directed toward advising the students in matters which will benefit them as teachers and idealizing the teacher's role in society for the avowed purpose of securing the student's loyalty to the profession. By way of illustration, the students are admonished to use "proper, dynamic, psychological methods of teaching." When this particular charge was given, there was no attempt made to explain or define this description of proper teaching methods. Much of the wisdom teaching is of a more homely and practical nature. The students in a general methods lecture, for example, were told, "If a teacher is punctual, children will definitely be punctual."

For the most part the training college lecturers are highly skilled orators. They speak with considerable assurance and style and very rarely find it necessary to correct themselves or search for words. At the same time, their use of English, the language of instruction throughout the B. Ed. program, is often stilted. This is shown in frequent grammar faults such as the omission of articles or the use of incorrect verb forms. Occasionally, the lecturers need to use an expression or phrase in their native tongue to amplify or elucidate a particular point.

The problem of student comprehension of English is even more pronounced than the weaknesses of the lecturer. The B. Ed. students have studied English as a foreign language for only four years at the secondary level, since most of the secondary schools use a regional language as the medium of instruction. In college the medium of instruction is English, and all of the students are required to pass an English proficiency test regardless of their major field. Nonetheless, students majoring in any of the Indian languages have considerably less opportunity to master English than those whose major is English or any of the humanities. Also, it is generally conceded that those with science and mathematics back-grounds are prone to have lower levels of English proficiency, ow-ing to the non-verbal nature of their studies.

Both faculty members and students were reluctant to show the written work of students, although there were no official reasons why notebooks, examinations and other forms of students' written work could not be seen. In spite of this reluctance, there were opportuni-ties to observe students' writings. The penmanship was considerably more uniform and legible than that found in the United States, and spelling did not appear to be the problem it is for many Ameri-can college students. Composition and style were weak, however, by seventh grade United States' standards. The students' responses to questions were not original or individualized and the writing was stilted. Nonetheless, when one considers the fact that English is not the native language of these students and that they have only studied it for seven years, this represents a considerable achievement.

The absence of original thought and inquiry seems to characterize the work of both the teacher and the taught throughout the entire process of teacher training. No doubt the use of English, a foreign medium of instruction, contributes to the problem, but it does not account for the fact that all matters are presented in a final, resolved, correct form, or that criticism, when it occurs, does not take the form of a debate over issues but, rather, is presented in the form of lists of faults or weaknesses to be memorized along with the other material in the syllabus for examination purposes.

Perhaps these problems can best be appreciated when one considers the fact that the Indian culture has only been exposed to Western scholarship for a little over one century. The emphasis on unity and conserving the knowledge of the past, two paramount features of the Indian intellectual tradition, might, for example, help to account for such training college practices as strict adherence to the syllabus and the stress placed on what appears to the foreig-ner as useless information rather than real problems.

The Indian penchant for preserving and integrating knowledge is clearly illustrated in the case of the educational psychology syllabus.[14] Here one finds human behaviour discussed in terms of "instincts" and "innate tendencies," and learning explained in terms of "transfer of training"—concepts that were prevalent when

[14] See Appendix I, The Bachelor of Education Syllabus, section on educa-tional psychology.

Bombay's first training college was established in 1906—along side the materials added to the curriculum in 1956, such as the Freudian concept of the unconscious or group psychology.

As a result of the great stress placed on unifying knowledge within the B. Ed. syllabus, the material is invariably arranged into categories or lists. For example, the students learn that there are "fifteen types of universities," "six ways to reform the universities," "four principles of timetable formation" "and five factors of discipline." In the course of a lecture this last category was enumerated as follows :

> There are five factors of discipline :
> Number one—psychological—good health—won't feel restless.
> Number two—growth (an explanation of this factor was not given).
> Number three—intelligence—low intelligence, can't follow, restless.
> Number four—social factors (no explanation given).
> Number five—management factor—comfortable benches, light, water.

The inevitable impression that much of what is being learned is not very useful is not limited to the foreign observer. The training college faculty and students alike expressed the view that certain portions of the curriculum were useless.[15] Specifically, this charge was most frequently levelled at the experiments in the experimental psychology course. Throughout the year the students are required to conduct fifteen experiments. A consideration of the following three representative experiments will be sufficient to provide an understanding of why these experiments have been the object of severe criticism.

1. Experiment to measure the fluctuation of attention—The subject is presented with a picture which alternately appears to be a white profile on a black background and a black vase on a white background. The number of times the subject's perception alternates during a specified period of time is

---

[15] This opinion was volunteered by several faculty members and students, but the proportion of each holding this view is not known. Faculty members would not express this view in the company of students and vice versa.

counted. This figure corresponds to the individual's fluctuation of attention.

2. Experiment to demonstrate division of attention—The subject counts from one to one hundred to himself, simultaneously writing the letters of the alphabet. The difficulty experienced by the subject in performing the two tasks at the same time is a demonstration of the effects of division of attention.

3. Experiment to demonstrate the effect of the distraction of attention—The subject is given a written passage and told to cross out particular letters in the passage. This same process is repeated while at the same time a distraction is introduced such as a loud tapping or the sounding of an alarm. The influence of the distraction is demonstrated by comparing the subject's performance with and without distraction.[16]

Although there is evidence of discontent with the present B. Ed. syllabus, very little, if anything, is done by way of changing or circumventing present requirements in the training colleges.[17] The staff of the training colleges somewhat resignedly accepts the inevitability of the system by which the syllabus, textbooks and the B. Ed. examination are controlled.

To a large extent the syllabus is based on the material in the prescribed textbooks, and the faculty members rely extensively on them in the preparation of their lectures. An examination of the fourteen major texts prescribed by Bombay University for the B. Ed. curriculum reveals two major characteristic weaknesses. Not only are the texts outdated as Table 12 indicates,[18] but the material in the textbooks, which is intended for a Western audience,

---

[16] W. N. Dandekar and V. K. Lothurkar, *Fundamentals of Experimental Psychology* (Kolhapur, India: D. N. Moghe, 1956). This text attempts to present a "lucid and simple presentation of experimental psychology covering the portion prescribed for B. Ed. or B. T. courses of different universities in the States."

[17] A training college faculty member from one of the training colleges outside of Bombay, who had studied educational psychology in an American university, reported that he was not able to teach the psychology he had learned there, because it would interfere with his main task of preparing students for the B. Ed. examination. For his own part he had to "re-learn" psychology in order to conform to the prescribed syllabus.

[18] The use of outdated textbooks often results in considerable difficulty in obtaining them. The librarian of one of the colleges reported that they had been trying for seven years to secure the prescribed hygiene text from London, which has been out of print since 1936.

bears very little relationship to the problems which Bombay teachers are likely to encounter.[19]

TABLE 12

PLACE AND YEAR OF PUBLICATION OF PRINCIPAL BOMBAY UNIVERSITY BACHELOR OF EDUCATION TEXTBOOKS, 1963-64

Subject	Place of Publication	Year First Printed	Year of Edition In Use
Educational Principles	London	1920	1930
Educational Principles	Bombay	1939	1955
Educational Psychology	London	1950	1955
Educational Guidance	New York	1930	1951
Educational Guidance	New York	1941	1941
Educational Guidance	New York	1947	1952
School Hygiene	London	1936	1936
Educational Administration	Bangalore, India	1951	1951
Educational Administration	London	1941	1941
Methods of Teaching Science	London	1925	1949
Methods of Teaching Science	New York	1940	1940
Methods of Teaching Science	London	1950	1950
Methods of Teaching History	Bombay	1940	1958
Methods of Teaching History	Bombay	1951	1951

Perhaps a more serious weakness of the texts than their being out of date is their lack of relationship to the Indian context, in general, and the urban problems of Bombay, in particular. Of the fourteen major texts examined, eight were written by Englishmen, four by United States educators and three by Indians. Where texts by Indian authors have been adopted, they have been written primarily with a view to conformity to the prescribed syllabus. Rather than relating the particular field under consideration to problems peculiar to India, they have summarized the work found in the Western texts which they have replaced.

As we have noted in the previous chapter, the evaluation of the candidates for the B. Ed. degree is based primarily on the university administered B. Ed. examination. The training colleges are only responsible for twenty per cent of the total assessment for the

[19] See Appendix V for a bibliography of the B. Ed. textbooks.

work in the theoretical portion of the curriculum in addition to their responsibility for assigning a grade for the student's work in the practical portion of the curriculum.

The B. Ed. Examination is divided into five parts, referred to as papers :

Theory of Education—Psychological
Theory of Education—Philosophical
Practice of Education—Special Methods
Educational Administration
History and Special Study[20]

The evaluation of the student's work in the practical portion of curriculum is primarily based on the faculty members' evaluation of the candidate's student teaching performances. In addition, the student's notebook in which he is required to keep a record of experimental work and notes on lessons that he has observed, is evaluated.[21] In practice, the assessment of practical work does not pose nearly the threat to the students as that provided by the B. Ed. examination. This is partly the result of the fact that failure in the practical work is rare, if it occurs at all.[22]

Failures in the B. Ed. examination, while not unheard of, are minimal, as Table 13 will serve to indicate.

A great deal of significance is attached to one's class standing. Employment prospects are brightened considerably by a first class standing, while a third or pass class standing seriously diminishes the candidate's prospects for employment by a prestigous and high paying secondary school or advancement to a supervisory or administrative position. As a result, the students devote the final two weeks of the B. Ed. program to an intensive review of textbooks, notes and probable examination questions.

There is a lot of competition between training colleges and students over the examination results. Practices vary slightly from college to college, but, without exception, a considerable period of time is devoted exclusively to preparing for the examination.

[20] See Appendix VI for a list of sample questions from the Bachelor of Education Examination.

[21] *St. Xaxier's Handbook*, p. 62.

[22] None of the training college principals could cite an instance of student failure in the practical portion of the curriculum.

TABLE 13

STATEMENT OF BOMBAY UNIVERSITY
BACHELOR OF EDUCATION EXAMINATION, 1963-64

Standing	St. Xavier's	Sadhana	S. T. C.
Distinction	—	1	—
First Class	14	10	6
Second Class	82	26	69
Pass Class	12	23	38
Failures	—	2	2
Total	108	62	115

For the 1963-64 examination, one institution prepared a mimeographed sheet containing all of the questions asked during the previous sixteen years, and all of the training colleges rely on previous examinations for review purposes. Perhaps the most extreme measure of all in this regard, however, is the practice employed by one of the colleges of administering a trial examination to all of its students in order to avoid, if at all possible, any failures on the actual examination.

This account of the operation of the training colleges has revealed many readily apparent shortcomings, ranging from the authoritarian approach of the principal and the faculty's unfavorable working circumstances to the colleges' characteristically pedantic approach to a largely outdated and irrelevant curriculum. These problems are compounded by the controls and limitations placed on the colleges in the form of the university-prescribed syllabus, textbooks and examination.

This is not to infer that the removal of the controls imposed by the university would result in the reforms advocated by the Indian government and its educational agencies. In judging the training colleges' practices by the standards suggested by the Mudaliar Report, it becomes obvious not only that the training colleges fall far short of meeting the aims set forth in the report, but, also, that the training colleges have not totally adopted these goals as their own. One is perforce led to the conclusion that either the Mudaliar Report is unrealistic or the training colleges are anachronistic. Stated in such bold terms the inevitable choice between establishing new training institutions and designing new goals for the present training colleges presents itself.

The solution to this dilemma appears to be taking a compromise path in the sense that more realistic goals are being established by and for India's training colleges, and, at the same time, new institutions are being created for the express purpose of training multipurpose teachers. These developments, which will be elaborated upon in the following chapter, suggest that neither the proposals set forth in the Mudaliar Report nor the accomplishments of the training colleges have proved satisfactory during the decade since the issuance of the Report.

CHAPTER V

THE EVOLUTION OF AN INDIAN SYSTEM
OF SECONDARY TEACHER TRAINING

FROM THEIR earliest beginnings to the present, India's training colleges have been the object of severe criticism. These criticisms have invariably been directed against the rote and superficial nature of the training program, in general, and the ubiquitous triad ; the syllabus, the textbooks and the final B. Ed. examination, in particular.

In retrospect, these features of the secondary teacher's training appear as a symptom rather than a cause of the training colleges' weaknesses. Nor for that matter can a realistic appraisal of India's teacher training problems be achieved through a critical analysis of any of the particular practices of the training colleges or all of the practices in combination.

In theory, India's system of secondary teacher training is as rational as that to be found in the United States. Perhaps, the practice of requiring teaching experience before entering the training program might seem implausible to the American,[1] but the Indian argument that prior experience enables one to derive greater benefit from the training experience is as cogent as the American view that one is unable to engage in classroom teaching without first having a course in the methods of teaching and a carefully supervised practice teaching experience.

Only when the more recent developments and present practices of the training colleges are seen in the perspective afforded by a knowledge of their history and traditions and the relevant administrative and educational context in which they operate, can one begin to understand the problems which these institutions face.

---

[1] *Teachers and Curricula in Secondary Schools* (New Delhi : Ford Foundation, 1954), p. 26. This report by an international study team is predictably opposed to the practice of requiring teaching experience before training primarily on the grounds that it encourages employment by schools of untrained teachers.

Hopefully, such an understanding will result in a lessening of the tendency of both the Indian and the foreign observer to be hyper-critical of India's secondary teacher training.

Just as there is no universal agreement as to what constitutes a good teacher training program, there is no universal standard by which a program can be judged. Perhaps the most judicious approach that a foreign observer can take is to measure a nation's progress towards its own particular goals.[2] In India this task is made relatively simple, for the educational goals are broadly outlined in the Five Year Plans and specifically spelled out by national commissions, educational associations and the officials in the National Ministry of Education.

Although differences with respect to means exist, there appears to be general agreement on the part of Western observers and Indians alike, that education should become more attuned to the needs of the society and, in particular, economic development.[3,4] This, in turn, calls for the expansion of the educational opportunities needed to raise the general level of education and the diversification of the secondary curriculum so as to include offerings of a technical and vocational nature.

Essentially, the multipurpose high school proposed by the Mudaliar Commission represents India's educational response to its need for social and economic development. However, in the ten years since the issuance of the Mudaliar Report, the multipurpose schools have failed to develop according to plan, not only in Bombay, but throughout all of India,[5] and the task of gearing education to an industrializing society remains India's foremost education priority.[6,7]

In order to understand why the goal of a diversified secondary

[2] This admittedly is a limited approach, for it assumes that the goals are determinable and that each nation's goals are appropriate for that particular nation.

[3] J. P. Naik, *Educational Reconstruction in India : Fourth Five Year Plan and the Role of the National Institute of Education* (New Delhi : Ministry of Education, Government of India, 1963), p. 14.

[4] Myron Weiner, "The Politics of South Asia," *The Politics of the Developing Areas*, ed. Gabriel A. Almond and James S. Coleman (Princeton : Princeton University Press, 1960), pp. 153-246.

[5] Interview with S. Doraiswami, Deputy Director, Regional College Unit, National Council of Educational Research and Training, January 28, 1964.

[6] Naik, *Educational Reconstruction in India*, p. 3.

[7] *The Times of India* (Bombay), March 14, 1964. The Union Minister of

institution has not been achieved, one must bear in mind the revolutionary nature of the Mudaliar Report. In a broad sense the yet to be realized multipurpose design for secondary education represents the rejection of the pattern of education which was established by Macauley's Minute of 1835 and has persisted to the present day. An education suited for only a small segment of the population is to be replaced with what it is hoped will become mass secondary education, and an education with an academic emphasis is to be replaced by one with a scientific and practical emphasis.

From a slightly different perspective the Mudaliar Report reprensents the persistence of India's reaction against the British educational legacy and an effort to create a truly Indian system ; one that is the outgrowth of the problems and plans of the Indian society.[8] The basic dilemma posed by the planned change is that the existing secondary schools and secondary training colleges are being asked to undergo a radical transformation—to give up the only practices and values that they have ever known in order to establish this new pattern of education.

Probably, the most basic obstacle to India's contemplated educational reform results from the social cleavages found in the Indian society.Traditionally, one's function in society and hence, one's position in the social hierarchy has been assigned at birth. The superimposition of the British system of education over the less formal yet clearly prescribed Indian means of socialization served to reinforce the rigidity of the divisions in Indian society by means of the introduction of an elitist form of education. Thus, the envisioned democratization of Indian education requires not only a rejection of the British system of education, but the traditional Indian social patterns as well.

India's residual caste system deters the amalgamating of a literary and humanistic education with a practical or scientific one. Throughout the history of Indian education during the British period, these forms of education have remained separate, and the

Education, M. C. Chagla, was reportedly considering a program designed to provide vocational training in the secondary schools.

[8] The extent to which India's educational plans truly stem from Indian thought and conditions is difficult to determine. Western influence and that of the United States in particular is, of course, great as the resemblance between the multipurpose high school and the American conception of secondary education amply attests.

proposal that they be brought together in the multipurpose school is perceived as a threat to the prestige of the academic high school. In a highly status conscious nation[9] an education in an institution that does not afford the maximum opportunity for entrance into the university is not likely to gain acceptance. Thus, one of the lacking prerequisites for mass secondary education is an acceptance of this type of education on the part of the people.

Events leading up to the present provide considerable grounds for doubt as to whether the central government can successfully bring about the conversion of existing secondary schools by a national fiat. It is true that, historically, the creation and development of India's educational system is largely the result of central direction. In particular, the actual establishment of Bombay's first training college in 1906 and its subsequent affiliation to Bombay University in 1922 were the results of the proposals of the central government and the allocation of the central funds required for their implementation.

One might be inclined to conclude that the mere granting of funds by the central government would be all that was required for the success of the Mudaliar proposals. The financial inability of the government to do more than contribute a fraction of the costs for the establishment of new multipurpose schools is, of course, a limiting factor in their development, but it should not be permitted to shield the other obstacles from detection, such as the lack of understanding or appreciation of the multipurpose schools, the lack of qualified personnel to staff these schools and the reluctance of the states to do more than cooperate with the central government's effort in a token manner.

The State of Maharashtra, formerly Bombay State, has been especially slow to cooperate with the central government's wishes in educational matters and the training of secondary teachers in particular. The last state in India to establish a secondary training college, it has consistently lagged behind the other states in the area of teacher training. At present seventy-six per cent of the secondary teachers in the city of Bombay are trained, but only thirty-seven per cent of these or twenty-eight percent of all the secondary teachers, have a B. Ed. degree.[10] Probably more than any other state,

[9] Myron Weiner, *The Politics of Scarcity* (Chicago : University of Chicago Press, 1962), p. 234.

[10] *Education in Maharashtra, Annual Administration Report, 1959-60*, p. 117.

Maharashtra relies on an examination in lieu of a training program to produce state approved secondary teachers.[11]

Politically, the states represent the first barrier against the central government's plans for multipurpose secondary education. Although the states have tacitly approved this design for secondary education, they have not taken the measures necessary for the training of multipurpose teachers. The continued state support of academic and technical secondary high schools provides further evidence to suggest that the states do not place a high priority on the conversion of these institutions to the multipurpose variety. Particularly in the city of Bombay, the policy of Maharashtra State has been to afford increasing support to the technical institutions rather than to adopt the multipurpose pattern of secondary education on a widespread scale. The policies of the state with respect to the support of secondary education can in part be accounted for by the state's reliance on the private societies' continued financial contribution. For the most part, the societies are neither disposed nor equipped to offer anything other than standard academic training.

The university, the agency of control for higher education, has similarly proved to be a major obstacle to the implementation of the Mudaliar proposals for secondary education. Through its requirement that secondary teachers be graduates of the university and its control over the Bachelor of Education curriculum the university has exerted a strong influence in the direction of an exclusive academic secondary education. Based on the influence exercised by the university since 1922, the year in which the Secondary Training College became affiliated to Bombay University, to the present, one must concede the probability that as long as secondary teacher training remains under the jurisdiction of the university, the prospects for other than minor concessions to the Mudaliar proposals are not very great.

Nor does it appear likely that Bombay University will establish a department of education, which is needed to provide the necessary institutional auspices for the specialized and advanced study of education in Bombay. It is perhaps partly as a result of the generally low state of the study of education as a discipline that the National Council of Educational Research and Training has developed the National Institute of Education. This institution is beginn-

---

[11] Interview with J. P. Naik, Adviser, Primary Education, Ministry of Education, New Delhi, January 24, 1964.

ing a two year Master's degree program and a three year Ph. D. course, in order to provide the necessary personnel to staff the training institutions throughout India. Eventually, it is hoped that there will be a sufficient quantity of graduates to staff the training institutions and administrative services in the event that the training colleges and universities do not develop advanced programs in education.[12]

The central government, which has played a leading role in the formulation of educational policy since the establishment of the British system in India, is today playing a leadership role in an attempt to create a multipurpose secondary school which will serve as an instrument for the attainment of national economic, social and political goals. The overall effect of the state's educational policy is that of retaining the existing system and expanding present facilities rather than acting as a force for reconstruction. Perhaps the university occupies an even more conservative position with respect to national educational goals than the state. Its primary concern for academic standards appears to result in a disavowal of any responsibility for the training of secondary teachers, except for those who are university graduates and are preparing to teach academic subjects.

In an effort to recapitulate the progress made in the secondary training colleges it must at the outset be acknowledged that their essential character has remained unchanged. To date, the training colleges have not only failed to provide the necessary diversified curriculum for the training of multipurpose teachers, but they have continued to function largely in the traditional manner that has characterized their operation from their earliest beginnings.

Nonetheless, throughout the history of the training colleges, and particularly since independence was granted to India in 1947, the training colleges have become increasingly oriented to the Indian society. At the time of the establishment of the Secondary Training College in 1906, instruction was restricted to Western academic learning. In 1922, a study of India's educational history with special reference to educational problems in modern India was introduced, and the vernacular languages were added to the curriculum as teaching subjects. With the curriculum revision of 1956, increased attention was given to contemporary Indian educational problems, and the curriculum reflected certain Western advances

[12] Naik, *Educational Reconstruction in India*, p. 16.

in the field of education as well. Probably the most significant change in the curriculum, however, was the addition of the special fields of education subjects such as guidance, education of the handicapped and basic education, for these subjects provide the student with an understanding of the application of a special educational program designed to deal with particular problems in the Indian society.

With respect to the methods employed in the training colleges, the theoretical portion of the B. Ed. program continues to be dominated by a more or less rote approach to the university-prescribed syllabus. Virtually exclusive reliance is placed on the lecture method to impart the material, and the primary motivation for learning appears to be success in the final B. Ed. examination. Nonetheless, the policy of internal assessment instituted in 1956, whereby the individual training colleges are responsible for twenty percent of the evaluation of the student's work, represent evidence of the university's willingness to overcome the excessive stress on examinations cited by the Mudaliar Report. Further, the testimony of the faculty members strongly suggests that the relationship between the faculty members and the students has become less authoritarian and increasingly cooperative in nature, thus creating a less formal atmosphere in the training colleges than was the case in the past. In the practical phase of the secondary teacher's training program increasing emphasis is being placed on the use of diversified methods to give increased meaning to the lessons. In particular, visual aids are recommended and the trainees are given instruction in both their preparation and use.

Not only are the training colleges slowly, yet perceptibly, moving in the direction of the goals expounded in the Mudaliar Report as far as the training of new teachers is concerned, but they have made significant beginnings in the task of introducing reforms in secondary education to in-service teachers. Through the extension program, a cooperative venture among the central government, the state government and the training colleges, methods and materials have been introduced to the in-service teachers that will enable and encourage them to implement the kind of reforms proposed in the Mudaliar Report.

The reforms in the curriculum, the less extensive reforms in methods and the development of a program for the education of in-service teachers are all indicative of the continuation of a gradual movement on the part of the training colleges in the direction of increased responsiveness to the Indian society's goals. But the key reform required for the establishment of multipurpose schools, the training of technical and vocational teachers, has not taken place.

The central government, which, historically, has had to bear a large share of the financial burden for technical education, found that despite its efforts (short of financial support) to persuade the training colleges to train multipurpose secondary teachers, the training colleges were unable to assume this task. Separate inquiries by the Ministry of Education in 1958 and a team of consultants from the Ohio State University under the auspices of the United States Agency for International Development (A. I. D.) in 1959 pointed out the need for both a clearer understanding of the purpose and the functioning of multipurpose schools, and an adequate supply of qualified teachers, particularly in the practical subjects, in order for the multipurpose schools to become successfully established.[13]

Based largely on these studies and the subsequent recommendations of India's *Third Five-Year Plan* published in 1961, the National Council of Educational Research and Training was charged with the responsibility of establishing four regional colleges of education for the preparation of teachers for the multipurpose schools.[14] However, the establishment of the regional colleges does not detract from the applicability of the Mudaliar Report for the existing secondary training colleges. The creation of these new institutions represents the central government's tacit admission that the Mudaliar proposals were overly optimistic, and that the training colleges' progress must be of a more evolutionary nature.

Based on the view that the training colleges are much more likely to achieve successful reforms when their future plans are the outgrowth of the collective will of the individual institutions rather than national directives, the National Council of Educational Research and Training has sponsored meetings of the principals of these institutions. Through the forum of an Association of the Principals of Training Colleges in India, plans for increasing the output of secondary teachers and including primary teacher training in the present secondary training institutions are now being formulated. Although the fundamental question of providing train-

[13] *Plan and Programme, Regional Colleges of Education* (New Delhi : National Council of Educational Research and Training, n.d.), p. 2.

[14] *Ibid.*, p. 3.

ing for teachers of non-academic subjects in the secondary training colleges has not been broached, the outlook of the training colleges is clearly being broadened by this national association.

It now appears that the central government is likely to contribute financially to the operation of the training colleges. The increasing willingness of the training colleges to perceive their tasks in terms of national goals and the promise of impending financial support, augur well for the future development of these institutions and the ultimate establishment of the multipurpose high school.

BOMBAY UNIVERSITY BACHELOR OF EDUCATION SYLLABUS [1]

THE CURRICULUM, which came into effect on June 20th, 1956, consists of five parts or papers as they are termed. These are outlined below, followed by the syllabuses for the various parts.

1. Theory of Education—Psychological

   (*i*) Educational Psychology
   (*ii*) Experimental Psychology and Statistical Methods

2. Theory of Education—Philosophical

   (*i*) Principles of Education
   (*ii*) General Methods

3. Practice of Education—(Special Methods)

   Method in any two of the following :

   (*i*) Method in English
   (*ii*) Method in Modern Indian Languages
   (*iii*) Method in Sanskrit
   (*iv*) Method in Persian
   (*v*) Method in French
   (*vi*) Method in History
   (*vii*) Method in Geography
   (*viii*) Method in Mathematics
   (*ix*) Method in Science
   (*x*) Method in Technical subjects
   (*xi*) Method in Commercial subjects
   (*xii*) Method in Home Science
   (*xiii*) Method in Agriculture
   (*xiv*) Method in Indian Administration and Civics

OR

Method in any one of the following crafts in lieu of one of the special methods (*i*) to (*xiv*)

[1] *St. Xavier's Institute of Education Handbook*, pp. 41-62.

   (*xv*) Cardboard Work and Book Binding
   (*xvi*) Leather Work
   (*xvii*) Cane and Bamboo Work
   (*xviii*) Needle Work

4. Educational Administration

   (*i*) School Organization and Management
   (*ii*) School Hygiene and Educational Administration

5. History of Education and a Special Study of any one Field of Education

   (*i*) History of Education in India from 1854 onwards
   (*ii*) One of the following Fields of Education :

      (1) Educational and Vocational Guidance
      (2) Child Guidance
      (3) Social Education
      (4) History of Education in India—Ancient, Medieval and Modern up to 1854
      (5) Education of the Handicapped
      (6) Basic Education

Paper I—Theory of Education—Psychological :

Section I

Educational Psychology

1. Psychology and its applications, with special reference to education.
2. Aspects of mental Processes.
3. The Innate Bases of human conduct—Instincts or Innate tendencies—Individual and Social—Their modifications.
4. The Unconscious : Repression and Sublimation—Some Freudian Ideas on Sex.
5. The Inferiority complex and some other complexes and neuroses.
6. Sentiments, Volition, Character and Moral Habits. The Will.
7. Play and play-way in education.
8. Mental work, interest and attention.
9. Learning, Remembering and the acquisition of Skills.
10. Transfer of Training.
11. Thinking, and Training in Reasoning.
12. Imagination.
13. Stages of child-development, with special reference to Adolescence.
14. Individual differences and their Implications for school work.
15. Backward Children, Problem Children and Young Delinquents.
16. Mind and Body.
17. Mental Hygiene, and Child Guidance.

18. Adult learning.
19. The psychology of the group.

Section II

Experimental Psychology and Statistical Methods

1. General Intelligence : Its nature and measurement—Types of Intelligence Tests.
2. Results and Uses of Intelligence Tests.
3. Special Abilities and their Testing.
4. Attainment Tests.
5. School Records and Educational Guidance.
6. Statistical Methods applied to education.
7. Collection and tabulation of Educational facts.
8. Measures of Central Tendency.
9. Measures of Variability.
10. Frequency Curves and Normal Probability Curve.
11. Principles of Correlation. (Only Spearman's method of calculating the co-efficient of correlation).
12. The new concept of evaluation.

> *Note :* With regard to items 6 to 11 above, stress should be laid on statistical methods ; students should be required to work out only easy examples involving the methods.

Practical Work

Simple experiments on : Intelligence, Association, Memory, Attention, Perception, Imagery, Imagination, Reasoning, Learning, Fatigue, Suggestion.

Paper II—Theory of Education—Philosophical

Section I

Principles of Education

1. (*a*) The meaning and philosophy of Education.
    (*b*) Education as a Science ; Contribution of Psychology, Sociology and Biology to education.
2. Aims of Education : Social and Individual Aims ; the Education of the whole man ; Formation of Character ; Education and Culture ; Education and Adjustment.
3. The Educational Outlook : School, Society, and the Individual. Education as related to nationalism and internationalism.
4. Different Aspects of Education : Education for leisure ; Education for vocation ; Education for Citizenship ; Education for emotional adjustment ; Principles of Social Education ; The New Outlook in the education of adults.

5. Education for Democracy with special reference to India's Constitution.
6. Data of Education : The Educant—the nature of the educant : Heredity and Environment.
7. The Teacher : The teacher's place in Education ; Qualifications and personality of the teacher ; Child-centered Education and the teacher as the guide and superintendent ; Teacher's Charter.
8. The Curriculum : Principles of Curriculum Construction ; Correlation of studies ; Curriculum in Basic Schools ; Curriculum and Social and Cultural activities.

Section II

General Methods

1. Foundations of Method—Child learning and Child expression ; Maxims of Methods ; Lessons—Units—planning and notes of lessons.
2. Types of Lessons—determined by aim and procedure ; Inductive; Deductive ; Drill ; Review ; Appreciation ; Laboratory ; Demonstration ; Radio Lessons.
3. Devices of Teaching—Assignment ; Questioning ; Exposition ; Illustrations ; Black-board ; Text-books ; Dramatization.
4. Devices of Testing—Tests, Marking, Examinations (essay type, new type).
5. Correlation of Studies.
6. Class vs. Individual Teaching ; Teacher—Personality : Discipline in classroom, securing and maintaining attention.
7. Educational Developments—Montessori and Kindergarten Methods ; Project Method ; Dalton Plan and Supervised study.
8. Methods of handling adults' class.

Paper III—Practice of Education (Special Methods)

(1) English

1. General : The position of English in India—its place in the curriculum and in life—the problem of bilingualism—standards to be aimed at.
2. Phonetics—The physiological basis of speech ; elements of phonetics with special reference to speech sounds in English.
3. The Organization of English-teaching in schools :

   (a) The stage at which it is to begin
   (b) Time to be devoted
   (c) General plan of distribution of work in English
   (d) Qualifications of teachers at different stages
   (e) Equipment (Pictures—library—self-work material) necessary for the teaching of English
   (f) Extracurricular activities with reference to English.

4. The teaching of English in the early stages :

(*a*) Approach and methods of teaching English : The Direct Method—the Grammar-Translation—their advantages and disadvantages

(*b*) Programme of work :

  (*i*) Oral work. Scheme for oral work and the methods for conducting it. Building up vocabulary and language constructions. Teaching pronunciation. Developing ability to speak as a basis for written work.

  (*ii*) Introducing reading and the Reader—Methods of teaching ; the mechanics of reading.

  (*iii*) Introducing writing.

(*c*) Reading (Text)

  (*i*) The purposes of teaching reading.

  (*ii*) Readers and the principles they should satisfy, with reference to existing series of Readers.

  (*iii*) Methods of teaching Reading—Silent and oral reading.

(*d*) Composition—Types of composition ; work in oral and written composition.

(*e*) Grammar—The syllabus and methods of teaching it.

(*f*) Extensive Reading—The Rapid Reader—School Libraries.

(*g*) Poetry—Purpose—Method of teaching poetry—Recitation—Kind of poetry to be taught.

(*h*) The mechanics of speech, reading and writing—Pronunciation—spelling—handwriting—methods of teaching them—correction.

5.   The teaching of English in the higher classes :

(*a*) Reading (Text)

  (*i*) The kind of matter to be read—Reading books and the principles they should satisfy, with reference to existing series.

  (*ii*) Methods of teaching Reading—Purpose and value of silent reading.

(*b*) Composition—Types of composition ; work in oral and written composition—The problem of correction of composition exercises.

(*c*) Poetry—Purpose—Methods—kinds of poems to be taught—Recitation—a study of a few existing Anthologies.

(*d*) Grammar—syllabus—methods of teaching the different topics—exercises—correlation with reading and composition.

(*e*) Extensive Reading—The Rapid Reader—School Libraries.

(*f*) Translation—purpose—methods of teaching it.

6.   Study of the courses in English prescribed for :

(*a*) English teaching Schools and

(*b*) Secondary Schools in general in the State of Bombay.

(2) Modern Indian Languages

Candidates are permitted at their option, to answer the papers on 'Special Methods in Indian Language' in English. (Marathi, Gujarati, Kannada, Sindhi, Urdu and Hindi).

1. Some cardinal principles of language learning, as applied to the teaching of the mother-tongue—the mother-tongue as a medium of instruction.
2. Factors in language learning—oral work, writing, reading and introducing to literature ; stage of pupil's development.
3. Aims of teaching the mother-tongue and standard aimed at in Secondary Schools—comprehension, appreciation, expression. Understanding the form and construction of the language ; planning for lessons in Prose, Poetry, Composition, Grammar, Diction, etc.
4. Language—Text-books as the chief means of instruction—Review of existing series.
5. Reading—its types—model, oral, silent, intensive, extensive, supplementary; Class libraries—Children's literature.
6. Composition—its various types and their suitability to different stages, Correction ; manuscript magazines.
7. Functional Grammar and Formal Grammar—their place in Secondary Schools ; Teaching devices.
8. Transcription and Dictation and their importance ; Orthography and good handwriting.
9. Purpose of poetry ; methods of teaching old and modern poetry ; Kinds of Poems ; Recitation ; Appreciation of poetry ; Preparation of anthologies.
10. Study of the prescribed courses in the mother-tongue in Secondary Schools of the Bombay State.

N.B.—In addition to the above topics, special problems connected with the teaching of any language should be dealt with separately, e.g. spelling, grammar and pronunciation in Urdu. Suitable modifications should be made when Hindi is taught as the National Language.

(3) Sanskrit

1. The aims and importance of teaching Sanskrit in Secondary Schools, its peculiarity.
2. Methods of teaching Sanskrit—(1) The Traditional Method, (2) The Translation Method, and (3) The New Method—their comparative study.
3. Graded course for the initial stage, Oral Work; Graded vocabulary; Picture Composition; Story Telling course for the initial stage.
4. Reading (Prose)—methods and material—kinds of exercises.
5. Poetry (Recitation)—methods and material—(Subhashits, epic and classical poetry).
6. Translation and simple Composition.
7. Grammar—Inductive and Deductive Methods and their relative merits,—Teaching devices; Different methods of repetitions; New Type grammar exercises.

8. Essentials of a good text-book ; Study of existing text-books and Supplementary Readers.
9. Study of the prescribed courses in Sanskrit in Secondary Schools of the Bombay State.

(4) Persian

1. The aims and importance of teaching Persian in Secondary Schools—The dual nature of the Persian language—A classical as well as a modern language—the difference between the two aspects from the point of view of grammar and vocabulary.
2. The principles of language teaching—Different Methods :
   (i) The 'Maktab' Method of teaching Persian—its pros and cons.
   (ii) The Direct Method—its merits and demerits.
3. Oral work with beginners—its scope and aim.
4. Introducing children to reading—the transitional stage.
5. The study of Persian prose—its aims—the species of Persian prose. The conduct of a prose lesson—exercises to be based on a reading lesson.
6. The study of Persian poetry—old and modern Persian poetry—its features from the points of view of language and thought—the conduct of a poetry lesson—difference of method between the prose and poetry lessons.
7. Composition :
   (i) Oral : its scope and function—the different stages of oral work—the problem of correction.
   (ii) Written : its scope and functions—the selection of themes—the problems of correction, spelling, handwriting and punctuation. Manuscript Magazines.
8. Grammar : Inductive and Deductive Methods—comparative merits—Place of functional and formal grammar. Teaching devices.
9. The problem of text-books—some existing series—their merits and demerits. Supplementary Readers.
10. Place of translation.
11. Study of the prescribed courses in Persian in Secondary Schools of the Bombay State.

(5) French

1. The value of the study of a modern European language with special reference to the study of French. The position of French in schools. The stage at which to begin. The standard expected in school.
2. The various methods of teaching French—their principles and their psychological bearings. Methods like the Direct Method, the Oral Method, the Grammar Translation Method to be studied in detail.
3. Equipment of a French room in Schools. Its value to the teaching of French.
4. Division of work : Initial stage—oral work—its nature, scope and scheme, phonetics. Transitional stage—Reading work—the choice of the Reader—

Reading lesson—Prose and Poetry—Composition, oral and written. Correction of exercises.

Advanced stage—selection and subject-matter for reading. Written composition. Extra-curricular activities found useful in teaching French. Correction work.

5. The place of grammar at different stages.
6. The place of translation in the teaching of French.
7. Use of aids like the gramophone, the radio, the cinema and dramatics in the teaching of French.
8. Study of the prescribed courses in French in Secondary Schools of the Bombay State.

(6)   History

1. Function and aims of teaching History in schools : cultural, sociological, ethical, intellectual, practical, national, international, etc.
2. Change in the outlook of history teaching in schools at different stages—Needs of the various age-groups.
3. An ideal syllabus :
    (i) Principles for selection of matter.
    (ii) Place of History : Local, National and World, Ancient, Medieval and Modern, Social and Cultural History.
    (iii) Current Events, Civics, Internationalism.
    (iv) Need for stressing the national aspects of Indian History.
4. Children's sense of time and place.
5. Organisation of contents :
    (i) Concentric, Chronological and 'Periodical'.
    (ii) 'Outline' study vs. Intensive one.
    (iii) Biography and Movement.
    (iv) Culture-Epoch Theory.
6. Methods of teaching History at different stages :
    (i) Narrative.
    (ii) Question and answer Method.
    (iii) Source Method.
    (iv) Dramatization.
    (v) Study of chronology, etc.
7. The Teacher—his outlook and training.
8. Illustrations and aids to teaching :
    (a) History Room—Maps, Time-charts; Text-books; Source Books; Historical Novels, etc.
    (b) Museums, Films, Excursions, etc.
9. Correlation with other subjects, particularly Geography and Literature.
10. Study of the prescribed courses in History in Secondary Schools of the Bombay State.

(7)   Geography

1. Place of Geography in education. Aims of Geography teaching in Secondary Schools—practical, cultural, etc.

2. Selection of subject-matter to suit the pupil's interests at various stages.
3. Scheme of work :

    (a) The Grammar of Geography.
    (b) Various aspects of Geography—physical, political, economic, etc.
    (c) Study of local and regional Geography.

4. Methods in Geography teaching :

    (a) Practical work : Field work; Appeal to imagination and thought; casual relations.
    (b) Map-making and map-reading.

5. Methods of instruction : Story Method; Journey Method; Inductive Method; Deductive method ; etc.
6. Aids to the teaching of Geography :

    (a) Geography Room and Museum.
    (b) Maps, globe, epidioscope, films, pictures, specimens, models, etc.

7. Correlation of Geography with other subjects, particularly with Science and History.
8. Study of the prescribed courses in geography in Secondary Schools of the Bombay State.

(8)   Mathematics

1. Aims and value of teaching Mathematics in Secondary Schools—utilitarian, disciplinarian, cultural, etc. The Mathematical outlook. Their influence on the syllabus and teaching methods.
2. Methods of presentation—Inductive, Deductive, Analytic, Synthetic, etc.
3. Importance of building concept. Experimental and practical work as the basis of mathematical knowledge.
4. Arithmetic—mainly utilitarian value. Experimental basis. Motivation. Practical life problems, Commercial method. Commercial Arithmetic.
5. Algebra as generalized Arithmetic. Shorthand of Arithmetic. Symbolic expressions. Formulae, Problems and Equations. Functional Teaching of various topics, e.g. Directed Numbers, Graphs, etc.
6. Geometry—Fundamental concepts, When should it be begun ? Three stages—experimental, deductive and systematizing.
7. (i) Theorems or propositions, (ii) Riders, (iii) Constructions.
8. How to present :

    (i) Congruence Theorems
    (ii) Parallel Theorems

9. Importance of Symmetry and Similarity in Geometry.
10. Early steps in Trigonometry. How to induce Trigonometrical ratios. Problems in Heights and Distances.
11. Correlation of the different branches of Mathematics with each other and with the other school subjects like Science, Geography, Drawing, etc.
12. Study of the prescribed courses in Mathematics in Secondary Schools of the Bombay State.

(9) Science

1. Place of Science in the School Curriculum.
2. Aims and values of Teaching Science.
3. Essentials of a syllabus of General Science for different stages of Secondary Schools.
4. Types of objectives for the teaching of Science and Criteria for selecting them.
5. Methods of teaching Science—Lecture, Demonstration, Development Method, Heuristic Method, Problem Method, Topic Method. Historical and Concentric Methods. The Card System Method. Contribution of the Dalton Plan and Project Method to the teaching of Science.
6. Correlation of Science subjects with one another and with other school subjects.
7. Visual aids and community resources in the teaching of Science:

    (a) Laboratory with its equipment for the teaching of General Science.
    (b) Visits to Workshops and Factories and fields in connection with the syllabus in General Science.
    (c) Maintenance of School gardens in connection with Nature Study.
    (d) Special problems and methods of Nature Study and General Science, Home Science for Girls' Schools.
    (e) School Museums.

8. Study of the prescribed courses in General Science in Secondary Schools of the Bombay State.

(11) Commercial Subjects

1. Place of Commercial Subjects in the School curriculum.
2. Aims and objects of teaching Commercial Subjects in Secondary Schools.
3. Methods of teaching :

    (a) Lecture ;
    (b) Demonstration ;
    (c) Inductive ;
    (d) Deductive ;
    (e) Problem ;
    (f) Analytic ;
    (g) Single Commodity Analysis ;
    (h) Historical Approach ;
    (i) Occupational Approach ;
    (j) Applied Economics Approach.

4. Different types of lesson in elements of Commerce, Book-keeping, Shorthand and Typewriting.
5. Aids to teaching of Commercial Subjects :

    (a) Picture, Charts and maps ;
    (b) Films and Filmstrips ;
    (c) Visits and tours ;

(*d*) Actual illustrations from the field of business.

6. Correlation of Commercial subjects among themselves and with other school subjects.
7. A critical study of the syllabi in Commercial Subjects for Secondary Schools.
8. Qualifications of a teacher of Commercial subjects.

(12) Home Science

1. The meaning and scope of Home Science—its place in a scheme of General Education.
2. Aims and objectives of teaching Home Science in multipurpose Schools.
3. Methods of teaching Home Science :
    (*i*) Discussion and Development Method;
    (*ii*) Demonstration Methods;
    (*iii*) Problem Method ;
    (*iv*) Project Method—the school lunch as an educational project ;
    (*v*) Special Methods of guiding practical work in cooking, sewing and housewifery.
4. Organisation of practical work :
    (*i*) in the school ; and
    (*ii*) at home.
    Supervision and evaluation of practical work of pupils.
5. The Home Science Department :
    (*i*) Its Location ;
    (*ii*) Size ;
    (*iii*) Furnishing ;
    (*iv*) Equipment ;
    (*v*) Storage space.
6. Aids to teaching of Home Science :
    (*i*) Illustrated material—samples, charts, modes, graphs, etc.
    (*ii*) Bulletin boards.
    (*iii*) Films and film strips.
    (*iv*) Magazine and text-books.
7.   (*a*) A critical study of the syllabus in Home Science at different stages of the school course in the Bombay State.
    (*b*) Principles of constructing different types of Home Science programme to suit the needs of different types of social groups.
8. The importance of field trips—their planning—execution and evaluation.
9. Correlation of Home Science with other school subjects.

(15-18) Crafts

Card board work and Book Binding ; Leather Work ; Cane and Bamboo Work ; Needle Work
1. The aim and importance of teaching Crafts in Secondary Schools.

2. Method of teaching Crafts :
   (a) Lectures on theory of the Craft
   (b) Demonstrations
   (c) Practical work
3. Study of the basic principles of the Craft and special techniques of Craft.
4. Correlation between Crafts and other School subjects, particularly Art.
5. Equipment of a Craft room.
6. Selection of material.
7. Care of finished articles.
8. Graded courses for different stages. The change in the standard of work expected at different stages according to age.
9. The place of working — drawings in the Craft work.
10. Importance of project work.
11. Need of stressing the Utility outlook.
12. Visits to workshops and industrial places in connection with the Crafts.
13. Study of the prescribed courses in the Crafts in secondary schools of the Maharashtra State.

   N. B. — Practice lessons shall be double-period lessons and shall be counted as one lesson.

Paper IV — Educational Administration

Section I

School Organisation and Management

1. Introductory :
   The scope of School Organisation, Management and Hygiene.
2. Social aspect of School Life :
   (a) The social life of the school and its nature
   (b) Organisation and government of social life in school like School Parliament, House System, Prefects, etc.
   (c) School Discipline
   (d) Co-curricular activities — Social and Cultural activities
   (e) School and the community, organising the Community Centres agencies of social education, the school as a social education centre
   (f) Training for Citizenship
   (g) Moral instruction
   (h) Religious instruction
   (i) Sex education
   (j) Rewards and Punishments
3. Academic Aspect of School Life :
   (a) Admission, classification and promotion of pupils
   (b) Teachers and classes ; Subject teacher and Class teacher ; rotation of teachers
   (c) Curriculum ; General knowledge ; Current Topics

   (*d*) Time-table
   (*e*) Home-work
   (*f*) Examinations
   (*g*) Co-education
4. General :

The Headmaster and his assistants ; Staff meetings ; Supervisory system ; Parental co-operation ; School inspection ; School records ; Progress Books ; Cumulative Cards ; Programme and Statement of Studies.

Section II

School Hygiene and Educational Administration

(*A*) School Hygiene :
1. The aim, objects and scope of Health instruction
2. Physical Education
3. Healthful school conditions :
   The site of the school — the school buildings — the class-room lighting, ventilation, sanitation and water-supply ; drinking water ; washing and lavatory arrangements ; School equipment —the problem of postures ; the Boarding houses; the play-ground.
4. Health service and supervision :
   Medical inspection — school clinics — care of skin, eyes, ears and teeth — signs and symptoms of infectious and contagious diseases peculiar to India — fatigue, mental and physical — malnutrition and its evil effects. Health Service Agencies — First Aid.

(*B*) Educational Administration :
1. Controlling Authorities — The Educational Department — Central and State : Universities ; Local Authorities — their functions and relations with one another ; Private Agencies.
2. The administration of Higher, Secondary, Primary and Social education and of Special Schools and Vocational Schools.
3. Provision and facilities for Training of Teachers.
4. New Concept of Education in India since Independence, as reflected in the constitutional provisions and Directive Principles.
5. The duties and functions of the Union Ministry of Education, with reference to the past role played by the Central Government under Lord Curzon since 1904.
6. The duties and functions of the State Ministries of Education, with reference to Bombay State.
7. Education in Bombay State since 1946, with reference to Primary Education, Secondary Education, University Education and Social Education.
8. The Grant-in-Aid code of Bombay State, as concerning Secondary schools ; Systems of Grant-in-Aid.

Paper V — History of Education and a special study of any one field of Education.

Section I

Outlines of History of Indian Education
from 1854 onwards

Introductory — Indigenous education and the state of education before 1854.
1. Woods' Despatch of 1854.
2. Establishment of Indian Universities.
3. The Indian Education Commission 1882 and its results.
4. Lord Curzon and his Educational Reforms.
5. Gokhale and his efforts in the cause of Compulsory Primary Education.
6. G. R. on Educational Policy (1913).
7. V. J. Patel's Primary Education Act of 1918 in Bombay.
8. The Calcutta University Commission.
9. Government of India Act (1919) — Education as a transferred subject.
10. A Review of Primary Education — 1910-1947.
11. Hartog Committee's Report (1928).
12. A brief study of the Secondary (Mudaliar) and University (Radhakrishnan) Commissions' Reports.
13. The National Movement and the educational contributions of (i) Sir Syed Ahmed Khan; (ii) Pandit Madan Mohan Malaviya; (iii) Mahatma Gandhi; (iv) Tagore ; (v) D. K. Karve.

Section II

One of the following special Fields of Education :
(a) Educational and Vocational Guidance
(b) Child Guidance
(c) Social Education
(d) History of Education in India—Ancient, Medieval and Modern up to 1854.
(e) Education of the Handicapped
(f) Basic education

Syllabus

1. Educational and Vocational Guidance
Need for Educational and Vocational Guidance—Individual Differences.

The nature of Guidance—What it is and how it is done. Its tolls (sic), technique and predictability.

Evaluation of Abilities and Interests—Intelligence, Attainments, Aptitudes, Temperament, Interests.

Methods of evaluation—Tests, Interviews, Questionnaires, Cumulative Records.

Educational Opportunities—High School courses, Special courses, College courses in relation to Vocations.

Opportunities outside the College—Educational Guidance and Vocational Guidance, Guidance at various stages of the child's career. Guidance in relation to individual difficulties. The general procedure of giving educational guidance ; the general procedure of giving vocational guidance—work of a Career Master in (i) disseminating Occupational Information, (ii) in testing children's abilities and interests, and (iii) guiding children in their occupations.

2.   Child Guidance :
   (i) The Concept of Child guidance
   (ii) The organisation and functions of a Child Guidance clinic—co-operation of medical, psychological, educational and psychiatric personnel for examination and treatment.
   (iii) The main types of problems referred to clinics : (a) Habit Disorders, (b) Behaviour Problems, (c) Personality Problems, (d) Educational Problems.
   (iv) (a) Psychological needs of children in the social environments. (b) Causes of Maladjustments in the home and the schools.
   (v) Methods of examinations : (a) Work of the Psychiatric Social Worker —The Social case history report. (b) Work of the Psychologist—The Psychologist's Report—The Intelligence tests and observations of other characteristics. (c) The Psychiatrist's interview with the child —through play, through drawing and through talk. (d) The Psychologist's interview with the parents and teachers. (e) The case Conference.
   (vi) Treatment and the underlying Theory : (a) Individual therapy with the child. (b) Group therapy. (c) Adjusting the Environment. (d) Remedial Teaching.
Students are advised to visit Child Guidance clinics and attend case conference.

Social Education :
   1. Social Education : The New Concept—its aims, meaning and content.
   2. Administrative set-up agencies for imparting social education in the State of Bombay.
   3. Community Development Projects and National Service Extension Blocks.
   4. The role of Social Education Workers in rural and urban areas.
   5. Psychology of Adult learning.
   6. Organization of Social Education classes.
   7. Use of Audio-visual Aids and Crafts (Handicrafts).
   8. Organization of recreational and cultural activities.
   9. The Library movement—Literature for neo-literates.
   10. History of Social (Adult) Education in Bombay State.
   11. Activities of the Board of Social Welfare.

   Note : Students who take this subject are advised to visit a few Social Education Classes.

History of Education in India—Ancient and Medieval and Modern up to 1854 :
1. Ancient India : Brahmanic and Buddhistic Education—their aims, ideals, features and institutions.
2. Medieval Period : Chief aims, features, institutions and contributions of Muslim Education in India, its principal patrons. Education of women in ancient and medieval India.
3. Modern Period up to 1854.

Education of the Handicapped :
1. Types of handicapped children : the physically, the mentally, the socially handicapped. Their characteristics. Magnitude and importance of the problem. Present-day interest in and approach to the problem. State legislation.
2. The Physically handicapped : guiding principles of the education of the crippled, blind, deaf, mute and double or triple handicapped children. Modern progress in the care and education of the physically handicapped. Follow-up and placement. Existing facilities in India/Bombay for the education of the physically handicapped children.
3. The Mentally handicapped : Their discovery and classification. Guiding principles in the education of children with low I. Q. problems of organization. Instructional problem. Special schools vs. classes. Problem of teacher personnel. Follow-up placement. Existing facilities in India/Bombay for the education of the mentally handicapped.
4. The Socially Handicapped : The delinquent child. A social and educational problem. Place of the educator and of the social worker in the re-education of the socially handicapped. Treatment and correction of delinquents. Special schools. Problem of organization. Instructional problem. Responsibility of the home and of society. Methods of preventing delinquency. Existing institutions in India/Bombay for the education of the socially handicapped.
5. General Problems : Training of teacher personnel. Curricular problems. Establishment of adequate clinics and special schools. Follow-up services and placement. Finance.
   Note : Students are advised to visit institutions for the various types of handicapped children existing in Bombay.

Basic Education :
1. History of Basic Education from 1937 to the present-day.
2. The Principles and Objectives of Basic Education.
3. The Sociological, Psychological and economic foundations of Basic Education.
4. Comparison of Basic Education with the different methods of activity education in the West.
5. The Basic School Curriculum—the physical environment, the social environment and craft as foci of the curriculum.
6. The technique of correlation as a method in the Basic Schools.
7. A Comparative study of the syllabuses for Basic schools prepared by (a) the Hindustan Talimi Sangh and (b) the Department of Education in

the States of Bombay, Bihar and Madras.
8. The programme of work in a Basic School.
9. Administration and finance.
10. The training of teachers for Basic School.
11. Post Basic Education and Secondary Education.
12. Research experimentation and evaluation.
13. Plans and Policies of the Union Government with regard to Basic Education.

PRIMARY AND SECONDARY ACADEMIC CURRICULUM IN BOMBAY

Class I-IV
1. Language
2. Arithmetic
3. General knowledge (general science, geography, history, elementary civics, health and hygiene).

Class V-VII
1. Regional language
2. General science
3. Arithmetic
4. Geography
5. History
6. Hindi
7. Craft work
8. Music
9. Domestic science (girls)

Class VIII-X
*1. Mother tongue (or regional language)
*2. Hindi
*3. Elementary mathematics and general science
*4. Social studies
5. English (or other modern European language)
6. Classical language (or optional subject for S. S. C. examination).
7. Art drawing or craft
8. Physical training
9. Social and cultural activities

Class XI
In class XI one of core subjects (designated by *above) may be replaced by one of the following electives :
1. Physics
2. Chemistry
3. English
4. Special geography
5. Special arithmetic

THE HIGH SCHOOL CURRICULUM PROPOSED BY THE MUDALIAR COMMISSION[1]

A. (i) Mother-tongue or Regional language or a composite course of the mother-tongue and a Classical language.
(ii) One other language to be chosen from among the following :
(a) Hindi (for those whose mother-tongue is not Hindi)
(b) Elementary English (for those who have not studied in the Middle stage)
(c) Advanced English (for those who had studied English in the earlier stage)
(d) A modern Indian language (other than Hindi)
(e) A modern foreign language (other than English)
(f) A Classical language

B. (i) Social Studies—general course (for the first two years only)
(ii) General Science including Mathematics—general course (for first two years only)

C. One craft to be chosen from the following list (which may be added to, according to needs) :
(a) Spinning and Weaving
(b) Wood-work
(c) Metal work
(d) Gardening
(e) Tailoring
(f) Typography
(g) Workshop Practice
(h) Sewing, Needlework and Embroidery
(i) Modelling

D. Three subjects from one of the following groups :
Group I—Humanities
(a) A classical language or a third language from A (ii) not already taken
(b) History
(c) Geography

---

[1] Report of the Secondary Education Commission, pp. 71-73.

    (*d*) Elements of Economics and Civics
    (*e*) Elements of Psychology and Logic
    (*f*) Mathematics
    (*g*) Music
    (*h*) Domestic Science

Group 2—Sciences
    (*a*) Physics
    (*b*) Chemistry
    (*c*) Biology
    (*d*) Geography
    (*e*) Mathematics
    (*f*) Elements of Physiology and Hygiene (not to be taken with Biology)

Group 3—Technical
    (*a*) Applied Mathematics and Geometrical Drawing
    (*b*) Applied Science
    (*c*) Elements of Mechanical Engineering
    (*d*) Elements of Electrical Engineering

Group 4—Commercial
    (*a*) Commercial Practice
    (*b*) Book-keeping
    (*c*) Commercial Geography or Elements of Economics and Civics
    (*d*) Shorthand and Typewriting

Group 5—Agriculture
    (*a*) General Agriculture
    (*b*) Animal Husbandry
    (*c*) Horticulture and Gardening
    (*d*) Agricultural Chemistry and Botany

Group 6—Fine Arts
    (*a*) History of Art
    (*b*) Drawing and Designing
    (*c*) Painting
    (*d*) Modelling
    (*e*) Music
    (*f*) Dancing

Group 7—Home Science
    (*a*) Home Economics
    (*b*) Nutrition and Cookery
    (*c*) Mother Craft and Child Care
    (*d*) Household Management and Home Nursing

CURRICULUM FOR THE BACHELOR OF ARTS, BACHELOR OF SCIENCE AND BACHELOR OF COMMERCE DEGREES OF BOMBAY UNIVERSITY[1]

Bachelor of Arts	Bachelor of Science
English and four voluntary subjects listed below :	One principal and one subsidiary subject selected from the following :

Bachelor of Arts	Bachelor of Science
English	Mathematics
Languages	Physics
Philosophy	Chemistry
History	Botany
Economics	Zoology
Sociology	Geology
Mathematics	Microbiology
Science	Animal physiology
Psychology	Comparative anatomy and embryology
Ancient Indian culture	Experimental psychology
Anthropology	*Geography
Politics	Statistics
	*Economics
	*Subsidiary subject only

Bachelor of Commerce

Principles of Economics	Statistics and Scientific Methods
Economic Development of India	Banking and Finance and any one subject selected from eight miscellaneous economic subjects.
English	
Business Organization	
mercantile Law	

[1] *Handbook of the University of Bombay*, Part II (Bombay : Bombay University Press, 1955) and *Handbook of the University of Bombay*, Part II, volume 2 (Bombay : Bombay University Press, 1963).

PRINCIPAL TEXTBOOKS FOR BOMBAY UNIVERSITY
BACHELOR OF EDUCATION PROGRAM, 1963-64

BROWN, JOHN. *Teaching Science in Schools.* 3rd ed. revised. London: University of London Press, 1949. (First printed in 1925).

GHATE, V. D. *The Teaching of History.* 5th ed. revised. Bombay : Oxford University Press, 1958. (First printed in 1940).

GHOSE, K. D. *Creative Teaching of History.* Bombay : Oxford University Press, 1951.

HEISS, ELWOOD D., O'BOURN, ELLSWORTH S., and HOFFMAN, WESLEY. *Modern Methods and Materials for Teaching Science.* New York : Macmillan and Company, 1940.

JONES, ARTHUR J. *Principles of Guidance.* 4th ed. revised. New York : McGraw-Hill, 1951. (First printed in 1930).

LYSTER, R. A. *Hygiene of School.* London : University Tutorial Press, 1936.

MOHIYUDDIN, M. S., and SIDDALINGAIYA, M. *School Organization and Management.* Bangalore : Government of Mysore, 1951.

MYERS, GEORGE E. *Principles and Techniques of Vocational Guidance.* New York : McGraw-Hill, 1941.

NUNN, P. *Education : Its Data and First Principles.* 2nd ed. revised. London : Edward Arnold and Company, 1930. (First printed in 1920).

RAYMOND, T. *The Principles of Education.* 4th impression. Bombay : Orient Longmans, 1955. (First printed in 1939).

Science Master's Association. *The Teaching of General Science.* London : John Murray, 1950.

STEAD, H. G. *Modern School Organization.* London : University Tutorial Press, 1941.

STRANG, RUTH. *Educational Guidance : Its Principles and Practice.* 4th Printing. New York : Macmillan Company, 1952. (First Printed in 1947).

VALENTINE, C. W. *Psychology and its Bearing on Education.* London : 1st reprint. London : Methuen and Company, 1955. (First printed in 1950).

SAMPLE QUESTIONS FROM THE BOMBAY UNIVERSITY
BACHELOR OF EDUCATION EXAMINATION, 1964

Theory of Education—Psychological

Assign psychological reasons :

We cannot apprehend all the letters ; rthiacsms together ; but we can when they form the word "Christmas".

Boarding schools are generally held to have a great advantage over day-schools in their power to establish a strong community spirit.

The process of suggestion should be unwitting on the part of the person receiving the ideas.

The playground is considered to be an uncovered school.

Explain role of following in moulding child's character :
  (1) Cultivation of appropriate sentiments.
  (2) Training of will.

Mention how a teacher should deal with :
  (1) a child with "parent" or "father" complex.
  (2) a child who has the "mother" complex.
  (3) a child who has the "inferiority complex".
  (4) a "backward" child.

Theory of Education—Philosophical

Describe importance of formulating aims in Education :

"Finally, all men are brothers, and the world is our home". Give one word for this outlook on life. State five ways by which you can help your pupils to realize this philosophy.

Education is a "bipolar process". Describe briefly the two "poles".

How are education and philosophy connected ?

Educational Administration

Select any four of the following cases and state how you would deal with them :
  (1) pupil who is habitually late.
  (2) one who always tells a lie.
  (3) one who neglects homework, forgets to bring books.

(4) who is generally disobedient.

How do the following contribute to well-being of school children :
(1) mid-day meals.
(2) Playgrounds.
(3) School medical services.

Educational and Vocational Guidance

How would you prepare and conduct an interview for students who want to prepare a vocational plan ?

What are personality characteristics—name any 5 that claim attention.

What does the term "guidance" mean to you ?

Why is there a need for Guidance ?

What services are to be included in a guidance centre in a school ?

APPENDIX VII

FACULTY INTERVIEW, BOMBAY UNIVERSITY TRAINING COLLEGES, 1963-64

THE FACULTY interview was conducted on an individual basis with twenty-four of the twenty-six faculty members of the three training colleges affiliated to Bombay University participating. The interviews ranged in duration from thirty minutes to one hour and twenty-five minutes. The informal approach of the interviewer, the open-ended nature of some of the questions and the interviewer's previous knowledge of the interviewee were primarily responsible for the variability in length of the interview.

1. Educational Background and Experience
   (a) degrees held—specify subject (s) and year (s) awarded
   (b) prior educational positions
   (c) prior non-educational jobs or positions
   (d) reason for choosing a career in education

2. Present Activities and Status
   (a) subjects presently teaching
   (b) hours of teaching per week
   (c) additional curricular assignments
   (d) extracurricular assignments
   (e) non-institutional professional activities
   (f) non-professional activities, e.g., other forms of employment or membership in civic organizations
   (g) research and publications
   (h) total yearly income from the above sources and any other sources
   (i) years on faculty, present rank, when promoted

3. Open-Ended Questions
   (a) What do you consider to be the most significant development in the training of secondary teachers in the last twenty years? When did it occur? Why is it significant?
   (b) What development or change in the present secondary teacher training program do you consider to be most needed?
   (c) What sources do you most commonly employ for keeping abreast with developments in your teaching field?
   (d) What are your career objectives?

113

BOMBAY UNIVERSITY BACHELOR OF EDUCATION
STUDENT QUESTIONNAIRE 1963-64

1. Age : ─────────────────────────────
2. Sex : ─────────────────────────────
3. Educational Background :
   (a) College (s) attended : ─────────────────
   (b) Degree (s) Held (circle) B.A., B.Sc., B. Com.,
       Other (s) ─────────────────────────
   (c) Class of degree (s) (circle) I, II, III ; I, II, III.
   (d) Principal college subject : ─────────────────
   (e) Subsidiary college subjects : ─────────────────
4. Length of previous teaching experience : ─────────────
5. Standards in which you have taught : ─────────────────
6. Jobs other than teaching that you have held : ─────────
   ───

7. Father's occupation ─────────────────────────
   Mother's occupation─────────────────────────
8. When decision to become a teacher was made (check one)
   (a) ───────────────── before college
   (b) ───────────────── during college
   (c) ───────────────── other (Please specify) ─────────
9. Subjects currently preparing to teach : ─────────────
   ───

10. Current sources of income (check where applicable)
    (a) ───────────────── Tuitions
    (b) ───────────────── Part-time day school
    (c) ───────────────── Night School
    (d) ───────────────── Other (please specify) ─────────

BIBLIOGRAPHY

PUBLIC DOCUMENTS

ABBOTT, A. and WOOD, S.H. *Report on Vocational Education in India with a Section on General Education and Administration*. Place of publication not given, 1937.

Bombay University Handbook, 1929-30. Bombay : Karnatak Press. 1929.

The Code for Recognition and Grant-in-Aid to Secondary Schools. Bombay : Government of Maharashtra Education and Social Welfare Department, 1963.

Great Britain. "A Copy of a Despatch to the Government of India on the Subject of General Education in India," dated July 19, 1854, printed in *Return of Sums Spent on Native Education in India since 1834*. Facts of publication not given.

Handbook of the University of Bombay. Bombay : Commercial Printing Press, 1937, Part II.

Handbook of the University of Bombay, 1922-23. Bombay : Government Central Press, 1922.

India. *Calcutta University Commission, 1917-19*, 5 vols., Calcutta : Superintendent Government Printing, 1919.

———. Central Advisory Board of Education. *Post-War Educational Development in India* (Sargent Report). Delhi : Bureau of Education, 1944.

———. "Indian Educational Policy Resolution of the Government of India in the Home Department," (Calcutta, March 11, 1904), *Progress of Education in India, 1897-98 ; 1901-02*. Calcutta : Director General of Education in India, n. d.

———. Ministry of Education. *Reconstruction of Secondary Education*. New Delhi : Government of India, 1962.

———. Ministry of Education. *Report of the Secondary Education Commission, 1952-53* (Mudaliar Report). 5th reprint. Delhi : Government of India Publications, 1962.

———. Ministry of Education. "Training of Teachers of Multipurpose Schools and Higher Secondary Schools (Government of Bombay)", *Proceedings of the Twenty-Sixth Meeting of the Central Advisory Board of Education*. New Delhi : Government of India Press, 1959.

———. *Report of the Indian Education Commission* (February 3, 1882). Calcutta : Government of India, 1933.

———. *The Societies Registration Act* (1860). New Delhi : Government of India Press, 1963.

———. Statutory Commission. Auxiliary Committee. *Review of Growth of Education in British India : Interim Report of the Indian Statutory Commission*. Calcutta : Government of India Central Publication Branch, 1929.

Maharashtra State. Directorate of Education. *Letter No. P. 14-R. 164.* Poona, India : May 12, 1964.

————. Government of Maharashtra. Education and Social Welfare Department. *Education in Maharashtra, Annual Administration Report, in 1959-60.* Nagpur, India : Government Press, 1963.

ORANGE, H.N. Director General of Education in India. *Progress of Education in India, 1902-1907.* Fifth Quinquennial Review. Calcutta : Superintendent Government Printing, 1909.

Report of the Director of Public Instruction, 1856-57. Bombay : Education Society's Press, 1859.

Report of the Director of Public Instruction in the Bombay Presidency, 1922-23. Bombay: Government Central Press, 1924.

Rules for the Secondary Teachers Certificate Examination. Poona, India : Yerauda Prison Press, 1958.

Sadhana Education Society. Bombay : Jawahir P. Press, n.d.

St. Xavier's Institute of Education Handbook. Bombay : William Printing Press, 1962-63.

SHARP, H.S. (ed.). *Selections from Educational Records : Part I, 1781-1839.* Calcutta: Superintendent Government Printing, 1920.

BOOKS

APPLEBY, PAUL. *Public Administration in India : Report of a Survey.* New Delhi : Government of India Press, 1957.

BASHAM, A. L. *The Wonder that was India.* New York : Grove Press, Inc., 1959.

BOMAN-BEHRAM, B.K. *Educational Controversies in India.* Bombay : D. B. Taraporevala and Sons and Co., 1943.

BOOCH, HARISH. *Pocket Guide to Bombay.* Bombay : New Photoplay Company, 1963.

CARR, E. H. *What is History?* London : Pelican Books Edition, 1964.

CORMACK, MARGARET L. *She Who Rides a Peacock.* Bombay : Asia Publishing House, 1961.

CURTIS, S. J. and BOULTWOOD, M. S. *History of English Education since 1800.* London : University Tutorial Press, 1960.

DANDEKAR, W.N. and LOTHURKAR, V.K. *Fundamentals of Experimental Psychology.* Kolhapur, India : D.N. Moghe, 1956.

Directory of Training Colleges in India. New Delhi : National Council of Educational Research and Training 1963.

DONGERKERRY, SUNDERAO RAMRAS. *A History of the University of Bombay.* Bombay : University of Bombay, 1957.

DORAISWAMI, S. *Extension Services Project in India.* New Delhi : Directorate of Extension Programmes for Secondary Education, Government of India, 1961.

Educational Activities of Government of India. New Delhi : Ministry of Education, Government of India Press, 1963.

Educational Investigations in Indian Universities (1939-1961). New Delhi : National Council of Educational Research and Training, 1963.

FAY, IVAN G. *Notes on Extension in Agriculture.* Bombay : Asia Publishing House.

FRASER, LOVAT. *India Under Curzon and After.* London : William Heinemann, 1911.

FURNIVALL, J.S. *Educational Progress in Southeast Asia.* New York : International Secretariat, Institute of Pacific Relations, 1943.

GORDON, D. S. *The Training of Teachers in Indian Universities.* Baroda, India : Inter-University Board, 1932.

HARRISON, SELIG. *India : The Most Dangerous Decades.* Princeton : Princeton University Press, 1960.

HEATH, KATHRYN G. *Ministries of Education : Their Functions and Organization.* Washington : United States Government Printing Office, 1962.

HEILBRONER, ROBERT L. *The Making of Economic Society.* Englewood Cliffs, N. J : Prentice Hall Inc., 1962.

Imperial Gazetteer of India. New Edition. Oxford : Clarendon Press, 1908, III.

India. Ministry of Scientific Research and Cultural Affairs. *Technical Education in India Today,* by L. S. Chandrakant. New Delhi : Government of India, 1963.

INGRAM, A.R. *The Gateway to India.* London : Oxford University Press, 1938.

KABIR, HUMAYUN. *Education in New India.* London : George Allen and Unwin, 1956.

KANUNGO, GOSTHA BEHARI. *The Language Controversy in Indian Education : An Historical Study.* Chicago : University of Chicago, Comparative Education Center, 1962.

MAGNUS, SIR PHILIP. *Educational Aims and Efforts, 1880-1910.* London : Longmans Green and Co., 1910.

MAYHEW, ARTHUR. *The Education of India.* London : Faber and Gwyer, 1926.

McCULLY, BRUCE TIEBOUT. *English Education and the Origins of Indian Nationalism.* New York : Columbia University Press, 1940.

METCALF, THOMAS R. *The Aftermath of Revolt, India, 1857-1870.* Princeton : Princeton University Press, 1964.

MISRA, B.B. *The Indian Middle Classes.* London : Oxford University Press, 1961.

MUKERJI, S.N. *History of Education in India (Modern Period).* 4th ed. Baroda, India: Acharya Book Depot, 1961.

NAIK, J.P. *Educational Reconstruction in India : Fourth Five Year Plan and the Role of the National Institute of Education.* New Delhi : Ministry of Education, Government of India, 1963.

————. (ed.). *A Review of Education in Bombay State.* Poona, India : Government of Bombay, 1958.

NURULLAH, SYED and NAIK, J.P. *A History of Education in India.* rev. ed. Bombay: Macmillan and Co., Ltd., 1950.

ODGERS, JOHN G. *State Bureau of Educational and Vocational Guidance.* Delhi : Kapur Printing Press, 1962.

PALANDE, M.R. *Introduction to the Indian Constitution.* 6th ed. London : Oxford University Press, 1956.

PALMER, NORMAN D. *The Indian Political System.* Boston : Houghton Mifflin Company, 1961.

PANANDIKAR, S. *The Teacher in India Today.* New Delhi : Ministry of Education, Government of India, 1957.

Parikh, G.D. *General Education and Indian Universities.* Bombay : Asia Publishing House, 1959.

Plan and Programme, Regional Colleges of Education. New Delhi : National Council of Educational Research and Training, n.d.

Rao, D., Dhupkar, G.H., *et al. Teaching Commerce in the Multipurpose Secondary School.* New Delhi : Directorate of Extension Programmes for Secondary Education, 1962.

Secondary Teacher Training. Paris : UNESCO, International Bureau of Education, 1954.

Shils, Edward A. *The Intellectual Between Tradition and Modernity : The Indian Situation.* The Hague : Moulton and Company, 1961.

Shrimali, K.L. *Better Teacher Education.* New Delhi : Ministry of Education, Government of India, 1954.

Shukla, Sureshchandra. "The Education and Training of Teachers in India," *The Yearbook of Education, 1963.* Edited by George Z.F. Bereday and Joseph A. Lauwerys. London : Evans Brothers, 1963.

Survey of Teacher Education in India. New Delhi : National Council of Educational Research and Training, 1963.

Teachers and Curricula in Secondary Schools. New Delhi : Ford Foundation, 1954.

Training Colleges and Examination Reform. New Delhi : National Council of Educational Research and Training, 1963.

Trevelyan, Charles E. *On the Education of the People of India.* London : Longmans, 1938.

United States Educational Foundation in India. *Handbook of Indian Universities.* New Delhi : Allied Publishers, 1963.

Vakil, K.S. *History of Training of Teachers.* Kolhapur : Shri Maharani Tarabai Teachers' College, n.d.

———. "The Secondary Training College, Bombay—A Retrospect," *The Miscellany of the Secondary Training College : Bombay, Golden Jubilee Souvenir, 1906-1956.* Edited by N.R. Parasnis. Bombay : 1956.

Weiner, Myron. *The Politics of Scarcity.* Chicago : University of Chicago Press, 1962.

———. "The Politics of South Asia," *The Politics of the Developing Areas.* Edited by Gabriel A. Almond and James S. Coleman. Princeton : Princeton University Press, 1960.

PERIODICALS AND ARTICLES

Bell, Reginald. "The Education of Secondary School Teachers in India," *All India Association of Training Colleges Quarterly Journal*, I, No. 2 (January, 1964).

The Bombay Educational Record. Vol. XI. Bombay : Education Society's Press, June, 1875, p. 124.

The Bombay Educational Record and Journal. XXI, No. 2 (August, 1898), p. 61.

Deshmukh, C.D. "The Crucial Issue in Indian Higher Education," *Asian Survey*, I (July, 1961).

"Forging National Unity," *Times Educational Supplement*, No. 2424 (November 3, 1961), p. 598.

GHATE, RHONA, "Indian Universities in Transition," *Universities Quarterly*, XIV (February-April, 1960), pp. 150-155.

JUNANKAR, N.S. *Asian Review*, LVII, No. 216 (October, 1962), p. 236.

Times of India (Bombay). March 9, 1964.

————. March 14, 1964.

UNPUBLISHED MATERIAL

Constitution of St. Xavier's Institute of Education. In effect as of 1963-64.

JOSHI, J.G. Address delivered at the All India Principals of Training Colleges Conference, Mysore, India, June 10, 1964.

Mimeographed list in the office of M.R. Bhise, Deputy Director of Technical Education, State of Maharashtra, undated but current as of May, 1964.

MULLA, A. H. "Difficulties of Secondary Teachers in the State of Bombay." Unpublished Master of Education thesis. Bombay University, 1954.

PARASNIS, N.R. and KHEDKAR, M.B. *Annual Report on the Activities of the Extension Services Department, Bombay,* for the year, 1963-64. Mimeographed.

SIDHWA, D.M. "The Training of Secondary Teachers in the State of Bombay." Unpublished Master's thesis. Bombay University, 1951.

Unpublished records of coordinator, Secondary Training College Extension Program, 1963-64.

OTHER SOURCES

Baroda University, Baroda, India. Interview with S. N. Mukerji, Dean, Faculty of Education and Psychology, April 23, 1964.

Bombay. Interview with Madhuri R. Shah (Mrs.), Education Officer, Bombay Municipal Corporation, February 20, 1964.

Interview with principal of a multipurpose high school, March 11, 1965.

Bombay University. Interview with A. Soares, Assistant Registrar.

Interview with A. S. Sthalekar, Chairman, Board of Studies of Education, May 7, 1964.

Elphinstone Technical High School, Bombay. Interview with A. G. Ghaisas, February 18, 1964.

G. T. High School, Bombay. Interview with J. Desai, Principal, March 13,1964.

New Delhi. Interview with A. C. Devegowda, Director, Directorate of Extension Programs for Secondary Education, January 25, 1964.

Interview with S. Doraiswami, Deputy Director, Regional College Unit, National Council of Educational Research and Training, January 28, 1964.

Interview with J. P. Naik, Adviser, Primary Education, Ministry of Education, January 24, 1964.

Interview with Sureshchandra Shukla, Central Institute of Education, January 25, 1964.

The Sadhana School of Educational Research and Training, Bombay. Interview with N. N. Shukla, Principal, March 4, 1964 and June 18, 1964.

St. Xavier's Institute of Education, Bombay. Interview with Professor M. Y. Bhide, February 18, 1964.

Interview with J. Mascarenhas (Miss), faculty member, April 2, 1964.

Interview with Father A. Solagran, August 27-30, 1963, September 27, 1963 and May 8, 1964.

Secondary Training College, Bombay. Interview with N. R. Parasnis, Principal, February 20, 1964, May 25, 1964 and June 16, 1964.

Sinnar, Maharashtra. Secondary Training College Extension Program Workshop, February 22-23, 1964.

INDEX

Wood Education Despatch of 1854, 8
   results of, 8, 9
   recommendation of Lancasterian
   method, 9,10

Xaverian Corporation, 65

Year Book of Education, 1963, The, 3